D1715774

RISE & FIND
An Ambitious Woman's Guide to Building Her Dream Life

eBook ASIN: B0DM6BM423
Paperback ISBN: 9798300942397
Hardcover ISBN: 9798300942472

Edited by Hilary Jastram

www.bookmarkpub.com

Independently published by #PinkFix Productions

Rise & Find

AN AMBITIOUS WOMAN'S GUIDE TO
BUILDING HER DREAM LIFE

DEDICATION

To all the women who made the strides before us to take us where we are today, finding ourselves and rising, rippling into the next generations to do the same and more. May we always embrace what it means to be a woman.

TABLE OF CONTENTS

INTRODUCTION

Over a span of 40 working years, women will earn $940,000 less than a man progressing through the same career milestones. To visualize this, I want you to picture the man sitting in the office next to you.

You and this man started at the company at the same time, rose through the ranks together, and now hold the same title and manage an equal amount of work. However, you will make almost one million dollars less than him during your career.

In addition, because you are a woman, you will have to do more work at home between childcare, balancing nutrition in an ever-changing body, oh, and don't forget to schedule self-development. If you take an extended maternity leave or attend to an aging parent, this number soars well over that one-million-dollar mark. Numbers that, as a female financial advisor, make my blood boil.

And . . . that $940,000 I mentioned is the statistic for a woman who works for 40 years and *only* takes the average maternity leave allotted in the corporate world. When you add in life factors like career breaks for longer maternity leave(s), caring for aging parents, or heaven forbid, time off to figure out your next career moves or just to have a mental health day, that number skyrockets.

Top it off with the fact that, as a society, we rarely see a woman as a whole person. I was reminded of this as I combed through my bookshelves. Several books told me how to sleep better, others advised on improving my health, and a mix of topics ranged from habits to relationships—but none spoke to *me*. I knew this needed to change.

As the owner/operator of a female-focused wealth management firm helping ambitious women and their families use financial planning to build their dream lives, day in and day out, I work with some amazing, trailblazing, and highly ambitious women. They, in turn, fuel my ambition. When I see a gap in the market like I did while combing through my bookshelf, my first thought is, *what can I do to change this*? So, I brought together the 12 most influential women I know, spanning a wide variety of industries, backgrounds, and lifestyles. All so we could build a guidebook tailored to you: the busy, ambitious, hard-working woman who deserves to be looked at as a *whole human* rather than just a piecemealed entity.

The title *Rise & Find* was born out of our mission as collective authors to help you rise up and find out who you truly are. Other books examine just one facet of your life and can leave you thinking you need to give up one area to go fix another. In the past, this messaging has left me feeling broken and often defeated, like I need to play small and hide the parts of myself I haven't read the guidebook on how to fix. The authors and I wanted to offer you something a little different

Our mission is to leave you feeling empowered in every part of your life. No matter what your life looks like.

You might be a high-powered executive in Manhattan, driving her way up the corporate ladder. Or you might be the CEO of your own company, trying to juggle it all while continuing to grow your brand and business. No matter your career or if you are a mom, caretaker, or are sandwiched between supporting these two (very different) generations, you will find yourself here. You are whole.

As you dive into this book, my hope is that you feel truly seen and heard for the amazing and ambitious woman you are.

In the coming chapters, you will dive into multiple ideas and topics, such as:

- Leadership tools that have helped one of our authors, Nora, stay ahead in a male-dominated industry.
- The power of women yielding wealth with Yahi and how taking charge of our finances actually changes the world.
- Equitable parenting conversations with Michele and a deep discussion on unpaid labor.
- An amazing legacy story by Lindsay that reminds us why estate planning is so important and should not be pushed off.
- The dynamics of being both a mom and businesswoman with Clara. (Whether you are running your own busi-

ness or in the corporate world, despite what the world tells you, feel empowered rather than ashamed to pursue both.)

- Tips and wisdom on the importance of travel for your family from Belkys, who knows that life is meant to be lived and enjoyed.
- While we laugh at being able to "do it all" in today's society, it drove Celina to coin her life-changing B.L.I.S.S. process to help you prioritize the most important aspects of your life.
- Which leads us to delegating and hiring out what needs to be done, and Jamie laying down the groundwork of the next and best steps.
- Don't forget to take care of the inside of you, too, and heal your past traumas. To move forward, you need to. Thankfully, Ilissa is inviting us to learn about HeartHealing.
- Trauma includes grieving, and Jaclyn bears her soul, retelling the gut-wrenching period that changed everything and how she came out on the other side into a new chapter of life.
- Briana underscores the importance of not giving up on your health to heal yourself holistically and continually care for the one body you have been blessed with.
- Bethany shares her inspiring journey of resiliency and how to build your brand and embrace what's coming at you rather than hiding from it.
- Finally, I'm giving you guidance on navigating the com-

plexities of finances and difficult financial conversations concerning multigenerational family planning, so everyone can understand expectations when building their own financial plans.

As you turn each page of this book, I encourage you to take what you need in this season of life. One fact is certain: we are all changing and evolving every day. Where you end up is in your control. The skills you learn here and elsewhere will give you what you need to make whatever you want happen.

I urge you to journal about, meditate on, and spend time with each of these women because they know you, they see you, they *are* you. Their pain and triumphs are yours and vice-versa, and when we share them, we are stronger together. We make a more resilient pathway for the women coming after us—and *that* is what being a woman is all about: rising and finding together.

CHAPTER 1

You Don't Have to Do It All to Have It All

Jamie Van Cuyk

"As women achieve power, the barriers will fall. As society sees what women can do, as women see what women can do, there will be more women out there doing things, and we'll all be better off for it."
—Sandra Day O'Connor

As women, we're made to feel that to have it all, we must do it all. Although our every success is a great accomplishment, and we often welcome each transition into the next phase of life with much excitement and joy, we must also face a reality each time we achieve something greater. That is the reality that each accomplishment or life change adds responsibility to our plate and rarely subtracts.

We don't climb the ladder of success. Instead, we advance to the next rung while still carrying the weight of every rung below us because we are taught to add to our responsibilities and never let go. We learn that success only comes when you show you can do it all.

Even worse, women are expected to accept this truth with a smile and not complain or ask for help because doing so must mean that we're not actually worthy of the level of success we've achieved. We're conditioned to believe that if we're incapable of completing all that is expected of us, the only option is to lower our position on the success ladder.

> **Success is exhausting for women and can leave you wondering if it's a myth that we can have it all.**

What if the real myth isn't whether you can have it all but whether you need to do it all to have it all?

Why Is Delegating Hard?

For many women, allowing others to help them is one of the hardest things they can do. Even when we know that we shouldn't have to do it all ourselves, we stop ourselves from letting go. Why is this? Why, as women, do we find letting go and asking for help so hard? As a hiring consultant who helps small business owners master the art of hiring and overcome their delegation challenges, I have found that there are three main reasons you might resist fully delegating at work and home.

1. It impacts relationships.

A study by Columbia Business School found that women resist delegating because they assume it can hurt relationships.[1] It is believed that you have to be aggressive to delegate successfully.

Delegating is different than asking for a favor, which may be confusing. It is true that when we delegate, we have to hold people accountable, and women who do so are often seen as forceful and pushy instead of as leaders.

This fear of changing the dynamics of a relationship or building a new relationship amid dread that you might be perceived as assertive can hold you back from feeling the joy of delegating. That's no reason to limit yourself. If you need to delegate, do it to the best of your ability, and know that it's okay to hold people accountable for the work they agreed to do.

2. Increased opportunity for mistakes.

The second reason women resist delegating is the fear that the person doing the work may make mistakes. They harbor the belief that no one can do it like them, so what is the point of delegating if the job will just be done wrong?

There are two truths to this. First, *no one can do it just like you* because everyone approaches the same tasks differently. It doesn't mean someone else's approach is wrong; it just means it's different.

---

1 To delegate or not to delegate: Gender differences in affective associations and behavioral responses to Delegation | Columbia Business School Research Archive. Accessed September 12, 2024. https://www.gsb.columbia.edu/researcharchive/articles/25937.

The second truth is *there will be mistakes*. No one is perfect. Throughout your career, you have most likely made small errors, like forgetting to attach a document to an email, or you have made other significant errors that have cost you or your company money or impacted a client relationship.

We all make mistakes, but that doesn't make us incapable. Don't let the fear of mistakes hold you back from letting go.

3. Being seen as a failure.

The last common reason why many women resist delegating is the fear of being seen as a failure.

Whether it's society or people we know, we are often told what it means to be a good mother, wife, business owner, or corporate leader. If you don't match the expectations set by others, you might believe they will see you as a failure in one or more areas of your life.

Delegating can create the fear that the person we are delegating to might be better than us. While we want the appointee taking over the task to succeed, we don't want them to do so well that it makes our accomplishments look like subpar work.

As a successful business owner or corporate leader, you might resist making moves for fear of showing errors in judgment or that it becomes known you did not perform at optimal levels during previous steps of your success journey.

But What Happens When You Don't Ask for Help?

While you might fear delegating, not delegating is not the answer. There's a cost to keeping all the work on your plate.

Let's look at the three downsides of not getting support when needed.

1. Deciding not to delegate accelerates reaching your personal capacity. There is only so much a single person can do. Refuse help and suddenly, your plate cannot get bigger to fit more on it.

2. Next, you'll start to disappoint others. When you try to do everything yourself, your work quality will eventually decrease due to time constraints. It could be that you're now always late with deliverables or that your work feels rushed, incomplete, or lacks in quality compared to what you used to produce.

3. Now, you're spending your time instead of your money, trying to chip away at the tasks looming over your head. While you might think you're saving money by not paying someone to help you, you're sacrificing your time. And that's just at work! Likely, you are also missing out on what brings you joy, or you're sacrificing activities that keep you healthy, like sleeping, eating well, and exercising.

Knowing that you should delegate is only the first step in removing responsibilities from your plate so you can focus your time and energy where it's needed. The next step is figuring out where you should start delegating your responsibilities. For some, the best place to begin is at work. For others, it's optimal to delegate at home. In both situations, there is undeniable value in getting work off your plate and freeing up your time.

Getting Paid Help at Home

When delegating at home, one of the first options people consider is delegating to a significant other, roommate, or child. While those you live with might be able to help, you have to be aware that their capacity might also be approaching its limit. Moving work from your plate to theirs just transfers the feeling of overwhelm to them. When no one who lives with you can take on the work that you need to get off your plate, it's time to recognize that you need domestic help and that it's okay to ask for it.

Paying for domestic labor can produce many unwanted emotions in women, including guilt and shame. Teresa O'Brien, the CEO of Help(her), a central Florida-based company that helps individuals and businesses check off their to-do lists at an hourly rate, has helped to address these feelings with many of her clients.

She notes, "I once had a client who was embarrassed to say she had hired someone to help with her laundry. I had to flip the script for her and tell her: 'You're successful at work, and it's because you're successful and know how to ask for help that you're getting the support you need. In addition, you're helping another woman by giving her paying work. It's a full circle, it's a win-win.'"

Helping her client realize that her success allowed her the ability to support someone else while also saving her time eased the shame she felt about delegating home tasks.

A few years ago, I had to overcome the shame of delegating domestic tasks myself. With two little kids, a growing business, a husband working full time, and busy weekend schedules, there was no time left for cleaning. Eventually, we hired a house cleaner. Not only did she complete tasks we were struggling to find the time to do, but we also had a house that was being cleaned all at once instead of piecemeal, which produced a calming, relaxing atmosphere instead of one always in chaos.

Getting Help at Work

While getting help at home is one option, most successful women also need help at work. Two ways to get more help at work are by delegating more to existing team members or hiring additional staff.

Often, team members beneath us are looking to grow and gain new skills to qualify for promotion opportunities. By delegating, you can help them improve their skill set while also enabling them to show up better in the areas where they are already an expert.

I had a few fantastic bosses before I left my corporate career to start my own business. One stands out above the rest because she let me own my knowledge and expertise. If there was a meeting with senior leadership about a subject I was knowledgeable in, she invited me to attend with her instead of trying to gather the information from me to present the data herself. Before long, my boss stopped attending specific meetings and let me go in her place. As a result, she freed up her time to focus on other responsibilities while allowing me to gain more leadership skills.

One of the issues that I find successful women experience in the workplace is they think they've delegated enough just because they have people reporting to them. Regardless of who's under you, if you're in a constant state of overwhelm at work, you have too much on your plate.

The Anxious CEO

A few years ago, I was brought in to help a company with 200 employees and over $30 million a year in revenue build a team for their new sub-business. While identifying what positions they needed in this new venture that would act as an independent small business, the CEO reflected on her position. She realized that feeling pushed to her limit wasn't due to the organization's size but because she was holding on to the decisions and strategic-level thought processes for all departments. By working together, we split her role into three full-time executive-level positions.

Had she delegated before? Yes. Was she delegating everything that she needed to? No.

Where to Start?

Once you realize you should delegate, you must determine what to delegate. Here are a few tips to help you determine what tasks you can offload from your plate. Download the Determine What to Delegate Worksheet to help you organize your thoughts and prepare for delegating success. Grab your copy at www.grow-ingyourteam.com/rise.

Step 1: Should you delegate at home or work?

The answer to this question varies according to individual needs. You might feel the right place to receive more help is at home, work, or in both areas of your life. To help determine the right place for you, start by thinking about what is getting in the way of having the time you want. Are you working an appropriate number of hours but stressed every time you walk in the door at home because of everything that needs to be done around the house? If so, delegating at home might be the right place to start. Or do you feel like you're stressed about work every day and can never get in enough hours at the office? If so, work might be the right place to delegate. If you're feeling stressed in both areas, delegating at home and work might be optimal.

Step 2: What should you delegate?

Think about what you want to delegate.

First, think about your current challenges or stress points. To help create this list, ask yourself these questions.

- What am I not an expert in?
- What takes up more time than it should?
- What limitations do I have because there's only one of me?

- What is constantly getting pushed off until tomorrow but causes stress because it's always on my to-do list?
- What are the items that must be done but I dread doing?

These to-dos could be anything from execution-level tasks, like creating marketing graphics or cooking dinners, to strategic thinking tasks, like determining marketing plans or making weekly meal plans that match your family's ever-changing schedule.

Then, for each item on your list, write how you, your family, your household, your company, or your clients would benefit if you hired someone whose primary job was to focus on that area.

Next, evaluate your list and determine which item would have the most significant impact if you delegated it. This should be what you prioritize moving off your plate.

When adding a new team member, the question is, should that be their only focus? To figure that out, evaluate the rest of your list. Any item that seamlessly fits into the core focus can be an additional responsibility of the new team member. For example, at home, you might be able to hire a personal assistant who will do your grocery shopping and laundry, but a personal chef would most likely not also do the yard work. At the office, an assistant might help with basic bookkeeping responsibilities, but a strategic financial professional who helps to ensure you're making the right financial decisions will not manage your calendar.

Step 3: Who should you delegate to?

Once you know what to delegate, you must find someone to take over your tasks. In some cases, it will be clear that you need to hire someone. While paying for help is something women should allow themselves to do, it's not always an option.

If you are considering paying for help, remember you can start small. A housekeeper who comes once a month is better than no help. In the office, not all positions need to be full-time. You can hire support at every level on a part-time basis. My first assistant worked 10 hours a week, and my first marketing team member worked 5 hours a week. You can even hire the skills of executive-level team members for a few hours a month.

If hiring someone is truly not an option, turn to your existing team. To ensure good morale with your employees, find the balance between giving team members more responsibility and expecting them to complete more work without proper compensation. If you're focusing on delegating at home, talk to your family members or roommates to see if they can take on any additional responsibilities. If you live alone, seek out a friend who could support you through bartering.

Yes, You Should Delegate!

You are a high-achieving working woman. You have worked hard to get where you are, and the truth is you'll probably need to continue working hard to achieve the next goals you set for yourself. That doesn't mean you must overextend yourself instead of getting help. Being in a place where you can delegate is a sign of success, so recognize that success and get yourself the support you need.

Whenever you are hesitant about whether you should delegate, ask yourself this question: "Does it need to be done by me, or does it need to be done right?" If the answer is "It needs to be done right," remember you can always hire someone and train them to do it right.

Let go of the work you do not need to do. This will allow you to enjoy the benefits of your success without constantly feeling like there's one more thing that needs your attention before you can relax. Enjoy your life by delegating and getting help.

To learn more about delegating and hiring the right support, visit https://growingyourteam.com/rise.

About the Author

Jamie Van Cuyk, owner and lead consultant of Growing Your Team®, is an expert in hiring and onboarding teams within small businesses.

Drawing from over 15 years of leadership experience, Jamie empowers women business owners and leaders to expand their unique businesses by teaching them to master the hiring process. Through learning each company's dynamic and specific needs, Jamie provides bespoke hiring frameworks and comprehensive guidance that helps women entrepreneurs gain the confidence to hire like a pro.

Jamie lives in St Petersburg, Florida, with her family. She is a hobby winemaker, loves to travel, and enjoys exercise that takes her feet off the ground, including rock climbing and aerial dance.

CHAPTER 2

Improving Personal
Prod-Tech-Tivity

Celina Mattocks

*"You should match your most important work with your
most productive hours."*
—Laura Vanderkam

I entered the airport lounge, sat down on a couch, and noticed a woman directly across from me. As a rolling robot came by to offer me a water, she patted her face with a napkin. *Is that a tear rolling down her cheek?* I thanked the robot. Her big brown eyes were red and swollen. She turned her head away from me, locked her laptop, picked up her purse, and dashed toward the restroom.

I thought about her as I set up my computer. "I'll be home late due to flight delays, babe. Please put the kids to sleep tonight," I texted my husband. The woman returned to sit across from me but still did not look well.

"Is everything okay?" I asked her, pulling out my earbuds.

She looked at me as if trying to decide her response. In silence, I watched her unlock her laptop, unplug it from the wall, and reposition it so I could see the screen. Ignoring my calendar alert pinging me about work, I curiously leaned in to see what she wanted me to discover.

It was a draft email. I read the subject line, and my eyes grew wide at her letter of intent of resignation. Right here in this airport, on a couch in a lounge, sitting across from me, she was quitting her job. *Was this for real?* I thought as I sat back on the couch.

"Would you like to talk about it?" I peered into her eyes. She closed the screen and nodded. I asked my virtual phone assistant to put my settings to *Do Not Disturb* with the message: "head down working" and turned back to her.

Her name was Taylor. She told me she worked for the very airline we were both flying that day. And that she was miserable and wanted out.

Taylor said she started as a flight attendant years ago and loved it. After a few short years, she was promoted to flight purser. "I was considered the top supervisor for each flight. It was a big step, but I was ready for it," she said, offering her first smile. Once she got the promotion, she transitioned well, was admired by her "airline family," got married, and eventually started a family. My watch beeped, reminding me to get up and move, but I silenced it.

This woman, who I had never met before, continued to bring me into her life. "The airline had a huge acquisition, and we've been merging and streamlining new systems," Taylor said.

"After my recent promotion six months ago to flight attendant manager, I became responsible for the work of more than 500 people . . . and now this system integration, which will theoretically make everyone's life easier." She frowned and shrank back onto the couch before continuing.

"I can't handle it anymore. There are too many problems to take care of in a given day. I have to push them off to extinguish the never-ending fire drills. I'm so tired when I get home that I'm not present and feel disconnected from my family. Morning, noon, and night, I check my phone constantly, waiting for the next disaster to strike," Taylor sighed. Just then, her phone vibrated, followed by an IM ding on her laptop. "See? It never ends." As she moved to check her messages, I suggested she ignore them and keep the computer shut. "These are merely distractions," I said. "Whoever they are, they will be fine without you for a while."

"That's just it," she responded, nervously tapping her foot. "I'm now conditioned to be 'productive' and 'speedy' in my responses. Work gets the best of me, and everything else suffers."

After a long moment of silence, she opened her laptop with gusto. "We have enough savings that I can take some time off to figure out my next step, indulge in a little self-care, and spend more time with my family. It's over. I'm sending this email," she said, moving her fingers over the keyboard.

"Wait! Don't push the button yet!" I said instinctively. "Taylor, have you evaluated how you currently spend your time compared to how you want to spend your time? Have you searched for your BLISS?"

BLISS

Bliss is defined as complete happiness and is synonymous with joy or utter contentment (Merriam-Webster[2]).

"Bliss?" she said, laughing. "I'm drowning! And the stranger in front of me is talking about happiness?" My watch gently beeped again. "Let's go for a walk while I share something with you," I said, locking up my laptop. Her eyes popped wide, and her mouth gaped slightly, but she removed her finger from the ENTER button on the keyboard and stood up to walk with me.

It was my turn to share.

"The BLISS model is a mindset and an acronym I use with clients. It's a way to help you be more productive and present every day. I don't use it to guarantee paradise or ultimate pleasure, but I use BLISS alongside productivity tools, such as digital diaries, calendars, automated marketing tools, and several sched-

---

2 "Bliss Definition & Meaning." Merriam-Webster. Accessed September 29, 2024. https://www.merriam-webster.com/dictionary/bliss.

uled online delivery services[3] to help me live a happier and more relaxed life," I said.

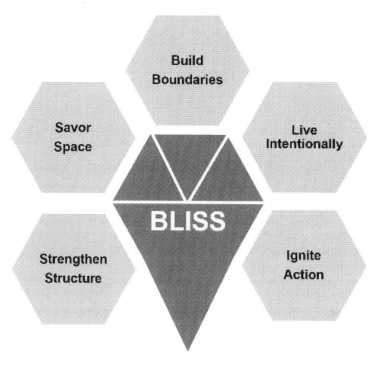

Figure 1. *BLISS Model*

As we walked the airport club lounge, I told Taylor that if she were amenable, I had five questions to get her into the BLISS mindset.

"I'm not convinced," she said with a shrug. "But go for it."

---

3 Free listing of recommended productivity tools (for Apple and Android) can be downloaded at www.leadlivelearn.com

Build Boundaries

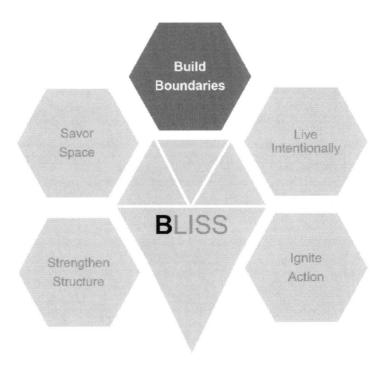

Figure 2. *Build Boundaries (first part of the BLISS Model)*

Most people know that boundaries mark the limits of a specified area. But many don't realize that they can increase their happiness and set expectations with those they care about by setting boundaries to be used daily.

"Question 1. How will you feel today, and how many new tasks will you get done?" I asked.

"I create emotional and task-related goals each day. It's personal for everyone," I went on. "But I recommend you decide your emotion for each day and choose a consistent number of new tasks you will achieve. Your choices become your daily boundaries."

I explained to Taylor that I use the Noom app to track my emotions, nutrition, and exercise. "For example, I set a goal to be energetic or calm, and I write it down here." I showed her the app's dashboard. Then, I switched apps to OneNote, where I showed her my six new tasks for the day and the six I completed the day and week before.

"These tasks can be the same type of activity each day, whether that's a work topic, thinking, home maintenance, and so on—but what you do or how you do it should be slightly different. Assume each new task takes an hour. You could learn a new Excel formula, read a different newspaper, try a different meal, or maybe experiment with a new cleaner," I said.

> **Delving into these processes helps you understand how long it takes you to do new things and how to get better at them.**

"Some people plan and document the night before, but I do it first thing in the morning. OneNote is a great digital journal with a sophisticated search tool that syncs to all your devices, which can be shared with others. These items become my boundaries to help me say 'no' to distractions that don't help me achieve my daily goals," I said.

"But how do you say no? Won't you hurt other people's feelings?" Taylor asked.

"It really can be so hard to say 'no,'" I agreed. "A mentor of mine once taught me that 'no' is a full sentence. I practiced 'no' statements repeatedly in multiple languages using the Duolingo app, although 'no' is quite a universal word," I responded with a mischievous smile. "Now, if I'm in the middle of working when I am interrupted, I respond with the earliest time I can help someone else. It's an important facet of time management, and your colleagues, friends, and family will admire your 'soft no' approach," I said. "It's time for you to give it a try."

"Where should I document this?" Taylor asked. I helped her download the app OneNote, where she created a new notebook called BLISS with a page for the week and a subpage for today's date. Taylor typed her desired emotion of *peace* and four tasks she wanted to accomplish. She winked at me with newfound confidence.

"Does quitting your job count as an important task?" she asked sarcastically. "It's quite possible," I responded with a little grin. "If you can't find your BLISS."

"Now, will you have bad days? Yes," I said. "Will you or your family get sick, and the list goes wayside? Yes. But your list is made to help you stay on track and build productive habits."

Live Intentionally

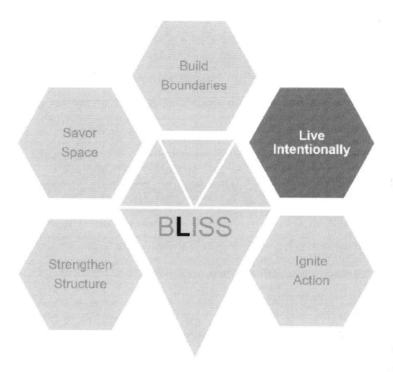

Figure 3. *Live Intentionally (second part of the BLISS Model)*

Many people walk through their lives without ever stopping to ask themselves, *why am I doing this*? Or *do I really want to be doing this*? Living intentionally means striving for congruence between your actions and desired results.

"**Question 2. On average, how many minutes do you spend in front of a screen each day?**" I asked.

> **We live in a tech-enabled world that can help and hinder our productivity. It's important to be mindful and in control of our digital habits.**

I showed Taylor how to check her digital well-being setting on her mobile device. She gasped when she saw the metrics on her phone: 2 hours, 49 minutes on average per day over the last week. "I check my phone multiple times a day, but I didn't realize it was that much," she said timidly.

"I sit in front of my computer nearly eight hours a day during the week and read my Kindle or scroll through social apps after the kids go down. That's almost 50 percent of my day," she said with a small, sad frown.

I told her that screen time can also be a symptom of a larger procrastination issue and to think about other ways she could disconnect.

"What quality time could you have with yourself or family and friends instead of being handcuffed to work?" I asked her.

Taylor took notes as we stopped at the lounge bar and ordered coffee from the kiosk. I suggested she access the Viva Insights app on her laptop to see how much time she spends in meetings, emailing, in focus time, and collaborating via chat. "I don't want to look because none of it is meaningful, and I no longer feel fulfilled like I used to," she said wistfully. I gave her an encouraging smile, and we kept walking. My watch told me we had walked 10 minutes and taken 1,200 steps. *Not bad.*

Ignite Action

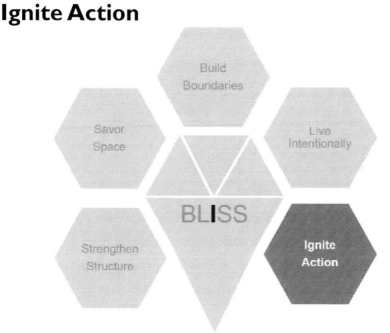

Figure 4. *Ignite Action (third part of the BLISS Model)*

Many people don't know how to take the first step toward their true desires, so they never do. If you make taking action a normal part of your life, the first step becomes immensely easier.

"Question 3. Each day, how often do you have a true sense of urgency?" I asked Taylor as I opened the airport app and requested an enclosed collaboration space.

"What do you mean? I live off urgency constantly," she muttered. I explained that John Kotter, the foremost authority on leadership and change from Harvard, defines true urgency as the desire to move and win *now,* and he claims urgency to be the most critical first step toward change.

Taylor's expression told me she was struggling to understand the difference between the urgency of her work and true urgency in life.

"You are about to quit your job," I said. "The urgency you have felt over the last six months doesn't feel like it's true urgency—like it's the desire to move and win, now. It feels like anxiety and being overwhelmed," I dared say as I led her to our newly reserved room.

Taylor followed and nodded, agreeing that she was constantly procrastinating on getting the important jobs done. "There are so many people and feelings to consider. Before my promotion, I only had one plane and crew to worry about. Now I move from meeting to meeting with an ever-growing list and no time to execute."

I asked her to take out her list and identify how many of her priority to-dos were work-related, to which she sheepishly answered, "One."

"From now on, aimless meetings are not the priority; the items on your list come first—and those items come now," I explained, reinforcing the importance of productive habit execution. "Structure will also help you," I said.

Strengthen Structure

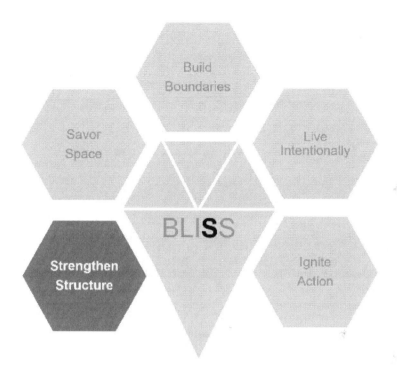

Figure 5. Strengthen Structure (fourth part of the BLISS Model)

Why is it so hard to find the balance between getting things done and enjoying life? Structure is simply about creating dependable time. During these consistently set windows of time, you can achieve your goals.

"Question 4. How many parts do you segment your day into?" I asked Taylor.

"Splitting up your day allows you to disperse your energy in ways that allow you to consistently win," I said. "Of my six important tasks, I complete two in the morning, two in the afternoon, and two in the evening. If I complete more tasks earlier, I'm done for the day." I shrugged as Taylor jotted down some notes on her cell.

I pulled out my tablet from my purse and navigated Taylor to my website. I showed her three dimensions to categorize her life priorities: personal, social, or environmental.

"These dimensions illuminate how you think about and treat yourself (personal), who you spend time with (social), and what information and lifestyle you seek (environmental)," I said, scrolling through the page.

I asked Taylor to review her new tasks. "I guarantee each item on your list falls into one of the three dimensions."

She calculated her list. "One task is personal—exercise using Map my Fitness App," she described. "One is social—make dinner with my children, and two are environmental—complete my final work product and finish my e-book while in the air."

"Great, now tomorrow try to balance out your life with a larger list in the personal or social dimensions," I suggested. "When you get home, you can take my assessment online to give you a full picture of your priority dimensions."

"But for today, let's use your digital calendar to place those tasks in specific time spots, color code them for visual cues, and mark them as busy." I pointed at her phone. "Once you get the hang of structuring your day, you can forecast and balance your week, month, and year with colors!" I exclaimed.

"You are way too excited about this productivity topic." Taylor grinned as she added four new one-hour appointments to her phone. I felt reassured as I silently watched her.

Suddenly, a voice came over the loudspeaker announcing that Taylor's flight was boarding. We left the collaboration space and returned to gather our belongings.

Savor Space

Cultivating three hours of personal space (physical, emotional, or social) for oneself each day is a leading indicator for highly productive people. It removes the too-busy excuses and turbo charges your mind.

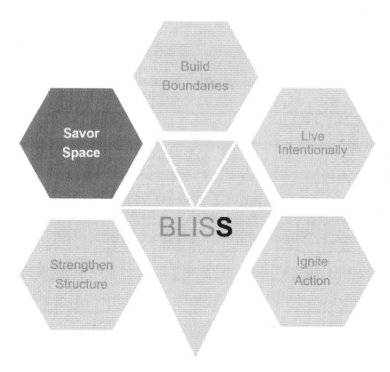

Figure 6. Strengthen Structure (fifth part of the BLISS Model)

"As we part ways, I have one final question for you," I said, and Taylor paused, zipping up her carry-on.

"Question 5. What are your favorite ways to relax?"

Taylor responded brightly, "Well, I love running or walking my dog in the early morning, baking with my children, or getting on a plane heading literally anywhere, but that rarely happens."

I know it takes work to carve out that precious time. Three hours of personal space per day sounds outrageous if you work full-time, own your business, or are a stay-at-home mom.

Taylor scanned the QR Code to access the elevator to the terminal. "Small wins can add up, like time to think, taking a shower or a gym class, happy hour with a friend, and intimacy," I said with a wink. "You are a diamond that needs to be cared for."

Taylor gave me a wide smile, and we exchanged numbers before the elevator arrived. I didn't know what she would do next, but I was glad to have met her. "Thank you for helping me discover my BLISS," she said as the elevator closed, and then she was gone.

"This is the single most powerful investment we can ever make in our life—investment in ourselves . . ."
—Stephen R. Covey

To get your free productivity tools checklist and download the BLISS Questionnaire, visit www.leadlivelearn.com.

About the Author

Celina Mattocks is an adventurous woman-in-tech focused on transformational change enablement at the C-suite and personal levels. She is the author of *54 Flights*, a short "coming of self" quick-read novel examining the life of a businesswoman searching for identity and contentment while pregnant with her first. Find it on Amazon (Audible, Kindle, and in paperback). Celina was named a past Top 100 Emerging Leader by Diversity Awards and has been featured on various podcasts.

Celina was educated at American University in Washington, DC, earning her Master of Science in Organization Development (MSOD). Her subject areas focused on intrinsic motivation and leadership alignment in mergers & acquisitions. She also attended Salisbury University in Maryland, receiving a Bachelor of Arts (BA) with a double major in Communications and Spanish—including a semester studying abroad in Sevilla, Spain. She is certified in Prosci as a change practitioner and in the Myers Briggs Type Indicator (MBTI) Personality Assessment. She is the founder of Lead Live Learn, a personal and leadership development company and is active in her local Washington DC Metro and Rockville, Maryland, communities.

Most importantly, Celina is a wife, mother of two, daughter, sister, and friend. She spends her spare time outdoors with her family and friends, reads self-help, and writes, runs, or practices yoga. She recently completed a personal development framework called Lead Live Learn, which aims to help others more in-tech-tionally live their lives. *Rise & Find* is her exciting second literary work. For freebies and training or speaking opportunities, find more information at www.leadlivelearn.com.

CHAPTER 3

A Diamond in the Rough

Jaclyn Hoffman

"You may not control all the events that happen to you,
but you can decide not to be reduced by them."
—Maya Angelou

As if starting a new adventure as an entrepreneur, being a mother of two school-aged children, and navigating life's busy-ness with a spouse working a full-time job on top of his own personal businesses was enough to tackle, discovering how to move forward after enduring a traumatic loss shook my life like an earthquake. It brought down the world around me.

In 2018, I severed ties with the corporate world after dedicating almost 10 years as a mental health counselor in a community-based setting, serving underprivileged, severe, and persistent mentally ill individuals. After gaining knowledge and skills as a post-graduate, I was excited to embark on a new path. I envisioned a private practice, having my own hours and *flexibility*.

I began as an in-home counselor for children and families as I pictured eventually hiring a team of clinicians to work alongside me. I diligently shaped this vision over many months. Partaking and cheering me on was my husband, Alex, who was not keen on my reduction of hours to part-time with a pay cut at first, only to quit that large mental health agency before long. Nonetheless, he was on board to see my dream to grow as a brand-new business owner with something to call my own.

Alex would sit across from me at my home office desk with his coffee in hand, providing support and encouragement in my new journey. He knew a thing or two about conducting a personal business.

Naturally, he had helped me get my business off the ground floor since personal businesses were in his family's blood. He was growing his own excavation company and establishing a small farm on what people jokingly called our compound, and he worked full-time as a police officer in our hometown. People say he was chasing the American Dream.

That Day

Death is something no one can ever fathom, yet it is a part of life we will all experience one way or another.

It was an unseasonably warm October day, with our children heading off to school, our oldest anticipating a track meet that mid-afternoon, me preparing to head to my in-home counseling job, and my husband going to his job digging out a basement for a new home construction—since it was his day off patrolling the neighborhood. I anticipated reconvening in the evening with a quick dinner, then schlepping the kids off to their black belt MMA class, watching a little television, and discussing our upcoming camping trip before turning in for the evening—like any other typical day in our household.

That supposed typical October afternoon was the day that my husband, a month shy of 16 years, my best friend of over 23 years, and the father of 13 years to one child and 11 to another, unexpectedly left this world.. Alex was only 40 years old when he died on that afternoon of October 2nd, 2019. Everything happening in my life up until that moment came to a screeching halt. I can still smell the burned rubber.

One can never fathom getting such upsetting news. But there I was, telling my children, who were also supposed to be having a typical day as they sat before me with smiles, sitting on their grandparents' familiar back porch. Their bellies were already full of ice cream in credit to their Papa, who knew their dad had departed and that their world would soon be rocked when they saw me. Papa put on his game face and distracted my kids toward something sweet in life for just a moment.

As I looked at them, my heart threatened to jump out of my chest, my eyes burned from intermittent crying jags, and I felt like I had swallowed a handful of rocks.

I uttered the surreal news that earlier that day, their daddy had died. In less than a blink, their eyes changed, and smiles drooped. I instantly knew the shattering of their innocent hearts. We were in a surreal place now. It was a moment in time that we knew we could never go back to, and we surely didn't know where we would be going. One thing was certain. Our lives were never going to be the same.

Damn, God sure played a cruel joke on my family that day.

I was now a widow.

I was now a solo parent to two devastated children.

I was also in the process of growing my mental health practice after breaking up with the corporate world, and my cheerleader had left the stadium.

What did I do to deserve this? What do I do now?

So many decisions were made not only at the moment of tragedy but in the days and months after. I made repetitive calls to family, friends, and even financial institutions, where I had to disclose the nightmare in which we were now living. I had to make decisions I never thought would come to mind, from how to have Alex's body prepared for his funeral and where to have his service to what to do as I combed through his assets and tried to manage his small growing businesses—all while trying to figure out my own. Furthermore, I had to manage not only my traumatic grief but the traumatic grief of our sweet children, who did not deserve to lose their father. Tasks mounted exponentially in the aftermath of Alex's death.

Nothing in the world prepares you for the loss of your partner, and as a mother and new business owner, I had layers upon layers of complexities thrown on top. I had to be a professional in such a vulnerable place. Me . . . a counselor?! I expected to be the beacon for my clients in times like this, but this beacon's light was now in a blackout.

The day Alex died, I was en route to see a client, and I had clients booked over the next several days. This tragedy was an unwelcome guest in my life. What could I do? Hanging a sign announcing I would reopen in the near future or allowing employees to cover my work was not an option.

My practice relied on me and only me. Paid time off for bereavement was not available, as I was no longer working for the man. Simply put, if I did not show up for work, I did not get paid.

One of the hardest things I had to think about was how I would be disrupting the lives of young clients who were already vulnerable and looking forward to our therapy sessions and with whom I had worked hard to establish trust. It was not easy telling them I was discontinuing my practice indefinitely, but I had to do it.

Thankfully, there were case managers I could inform to support these clients as they continued their therapy with a new practitioner. It was the best I could do in navigating my crisis. I had to focus on caring for myself in any capacity while showing up for my children and easing their worries about losing our home. Furthermore, as their only parent, I had to establish and implement a new routine for them as they prepared to transition back to school after taking time off for bereavement.

When dealing with grief, parenting, and growing a small business, prioritizing is crucial. Self-care came in the form of resting when I had to, especially because grief is emotionally and physically taxing. I would acknowledge my feelings of grief, which included anger, sadness, fear, and confusion. I know these emotions are all valid and will make themselves at home with me for a good long while.

For several months, I admit that I yelled, cried, and, yes, broke things. My sleep was out of sorts from being up for hours at a time in a quiet bed. My appetite was quite suppressed, and it took several weeks to get back to a normal meal and sleep routine. In those early moments of grief, I let myself feel what I needed to and did my best to balance all the rest. This is my grief and my journey.

I want to acknowledge that grief will look different for everyone. The early onset of grief to its manifestation months or years later can look and feel very different. Your journey with grief is yours alone.

COVID Didn't Shake Me

It goes without saying that life was rather normal for many up until early 2020, when the pandemic made the world go dark. Because I had lost Alex, I was a step ahead of those enduring traumatic losses and abrupt changes to their small businesses.

I felt incredibly fortunate that I could take the time from October 2019 through 2020 to revisit my intention of getting back into private practice versus trying to secure a job to keep things afloat. I gratefully took that time and allowed it to help me process, reflect, and figure out how to regain some footing in my "new, not-so-normal life." I knew I had to let myself be.

I had so many questions resulting from exploring various avenues to process my grief and trauma. I had put my nose in various books related to grief and spirituality. I had textbook grief down to a science from years of clinical work.-But there had to be more to *this life* than living, loving our people, and then losing them to death, right?

I cannot relate to grieving over the passing of a parent, sibling, or child, but I can relate to losing someone incredibly special in your life and how it can make you question the true meaning of life and be painful, fear-inducing, and victimizing.

Many months after Alex's passing, I still had profound questions that needed satisfying answers. Despite those yearning questions and the heartache and adjustments I had to make moving forward, I discovered so much more about myself and poured it into both my personal and professional life. I fell into energy work, visited desensitization tanks for solitude and self-reflection, and practiced meditation and Reiki, amongst other supportive modalities that helped me restore my being and nourish my soul.

I became my own client and worked on rediscovering myself.

I chose not to rush back into getting my business up and running but rather trusted the process of where I was at that moment and what opportunities lay before me. I let my emotions flow when needed, and if it meant I was sad, angry, or confused, I honored the intensity of each, as well as the peace that followed. After all, how can I encourage my clients to sit with their grief experiences if I didn't do the same with mine? Mind you, this is even months and years after losing my husband.

Random run-ins with former clients at a local store asking when I would return to my practice was a nudge by the universe to get back to my purpose. After a few phone calls inquiring about my services and a little more time, I showed up for clients again at my own pace.

My renewed practice transitioned from virtual sessions in my home office to car therapy at a local Target shopping center to meeting an old high school classmate for an acupuncture session and her offer to let me use space in her office to provide in-person counseling. She smiled. "I need someone like you here." I express gratitude for so many opportunities I encounter, knowing it is not just a coincidence but *synchronicity*. As each opportunity reveals itself, it affirms it is time for me to rise & find myself!

I refuse to let fear consume me. However, we can be fearful of change, especially when things have been Kosher for many years. Alex and I had a great system as a couple and parents of over 15 and 13 years, respectively. It might not have always been flawless, but when things weren't going according to plan, we problem-solved and figured it out.

If I had a penny for every time I thought to myself, *what do I do now*? Or *how can I go on*? I would probably not have to worry about money ever again. Okay, slight exaggeration, but I did let those thoughts consume me enough that I created unnecessary anxiety and depression as I dwelled on what the future would be like or held onto the past I no longer had.

Uncertainty of whether I was making the right decision to stay with my small business still crept in from time to time. The worst part is when it comes in the middle of the night, and your brain just won't shut off. I told fear to take a chill pill and trusted that if I was going to grow, I had to get out of my comfort zone. I chose to take the path of entrepreneurship and stayed with it, trusting that my intuition was working toward surrendering to it. In all, the best thing for me was to resume my practice, but it is 100% okay if this decision is not a fit for everyone.

I believe we are all capable of making something beautiful, even out of a tragedy like the one I endured. While I miss my beloved Alex with every ounce of my being, I have learned to embrace opportunities and am working toward being less fearful about who I want to be. And I still appreciate every possibility that comes my way. In my heart, I know that is what Alex would want me to do.

I can still envision him sitting across from my office desk, his coffee in hand as he coaches me. More importantly, I have our two children to consider. Parenting is not an easy feat now that I have to navigate the teenage years without their father, but I am learning that leaning on others for support when it is needed is more than okay.

When others continue to acknowledge your loved one, it adds to the healing process. The resiliency I demonstrate in front of my children leads to my hope that they will be encouraged to persevere in their own challenging times. I have much gratitude for my family and friends who have supported us along the way as well.

I know the world is mine for the taking, just as it's yours! Having grace has taught me so much on this journey. When things become too heavy to bear, I acknowledge it and put whatever I am carrying down to rest. Have faith that it is okay to slow down. The truth is, you'll never have it all figured out anyway, so trust the process.

Grief is not immune to any of us. I cannot stress enough that we all will experience grief in our own way. I explain to my clients that you cannot compare your loss to another individual's. How you handle grief is on your terms, and as long as there are no maladaptive coping tools like trying to harm yourself, alcohol abuse, or other substance use, chances are you are on the better track for healing. However, if you are struggling in a way that needs more professional attention, lean in and take the support. An abundance of hotlines is available to support you, like SAMHSA (Substance Abuse and Mental Health Services Administration) at 1-800-662-HELP.

The reality about grief is this—*you will never be the old you. She is no longer there.* You can try with all your might to find her, but another part of grieving the loss of your spouse is also grieving who you *were.* My role as a wife was ripped from me on that tragic October day.

Chances are, you will feel victimized. Losing Alex made me question what I did to deserve losing someone. I felt punished by my higher power. I felt vulnerable and exposed, especially in a small town where Alex had an influential role in the community, including when I read anti-police statements by those who knew nothing about him and their absurd comments about how he died. I became a keyboard warrior in some of those moments, defending his image, but eventually realized people are going to make assumptions. I was probably better off putting my energy toward something more productive, like healing and supporting my children and myself.

I would never wish my experience on my worst enemy, but I have found over time that my grief journey has made me a more authentic person.

I seized new opportunities when I could, including new hobbies, and I was open to the possibility that happiness could come back into my life. With that, I felt less fearful and less guilt.

I have no doubt that working to heal my grief also helped my children manage theirs. This was no easy feat for them, and I am proud to see how my children continue to move through this with perseverance and resiliency.

Again, if you are in the thick of it, do not be afraid of seeking the help of a professional, even if it is your local parishioner, a friend, or a family member. You can attend grief groups both in person and on social media. There is something to be said about talking with others on a similar journey. They welcome you to the club that you never wanted to join.

Almost five years after losing Alex, I am now venturing into the realm of coaching widows and helping them reinvent their shattered lives so they can feel guiltless and fearless moving forward. As I resonate with other widows, I provide individual and group coaching, where people can learn together through mind, body, and spirit to nurture themselves, get unstuck, and surge toward the life they deserve. You can learn more about my work at www.jaclynhoffman.com, @soulfuljourney55 on Instagram, and SoulfulJourney55 on Facebook. Widows are invited to an exclusive Facebook group, **Igniting the Phoenix Within**, which provides nourishing content to empower the widow.

About the Author

Jaclyn Hoffman is a grief specialist supporting early widows by empowering them to redefine their lives after loss through self-care, parenting, and pursuing new relationships. With almost two decades of clinical experience, Jaclyn has led countless women through their journey of healing and self-discovery through individual and group work. She holds two master's degrees in General Psychology and Mental Health Counseling.

Jaclyn describes herself as a perpetual student at heart and incorporates specialized areas of griefwork while integrating energy work like Reiki. When not coaching, she enjoys venturing outdoors in the woods or at the beach, studying the metaphysical sciences, and homesteading with her chickens, sheep, and honeybees. She takes on DIY projects for health and wellness and revels in planning camping adventures with her two sons and dog, Zen. You can learn more about Jaclyn's work by visiting her website at www.jaclynhoffman.com.

CHAPTER 4

A Life Well Planned: Barbara's Story

Lindsay Wheeler

"You only live once, but if you do it right, once is enough."
—Mae West

L et me tell you a story about a woman named Barbara. She was an amazing human. The best you could have ever met. Barbara was born in El Paso, Texas, on October 28, 1929, the day before Black Tuesday when the stock market crashed, and the US entered into the Great Depression. This would shape her life as a woman of determination, resilience, and kindness.

As a small child, Barbara would frequently take trips across to border into Chihuahua, Mexico, with her father.

Before she was born, her father was known for helping to smuggle supplies to the Mexican revolutionary Pancho Villa. Often on their trips across the border, locals would yell to Barbara, who they called "Dutchess," and her father, whom they referred to as "The Duke," "Viva Pancho!" They would raise their fists in solidarity for the fallen general. Later, Barbara would cross over to Mexico to meet up with soldiers wanting to party before they were shipped out. She was fluent in Spanish from her travels back and forth between the borders and would often slip between the two languages.

Later, when Barbara was a young woman, she would marry a man named Jimmy. On the nights when Barbara cooked dinner for some of us neighborhood kids, she would reminisce about her marriage to him. She said it was love at first sight when he stepped onto the city bus she was riding to school that day. Jimmy was handsome, and they would go on to have a son, David, two years later.

Barbara wasn't fully certain as to what exactly Jimmy did for work since he was such a free spirit. Similar to her father, Jimmy was absent from the family and traveled a lot "for work" but would send envelopes of cash when he could. For some reason, this never really bothered her; maybe all those trips across the border with her father gave her a more laissez-faire attitude about such things. Although, she would comment with a tinge of irritation about being primarily left alone to raise David. Barbara would tell us with a hint of mischief that curiously, Jimmy was on the last flight out of Cuba before the revolution. Jimmy said that she was the love of his life, but just not in this life. They would soon divorce. I don't think she had any ill will toward him for his lifestyle and abandoning her with a child; such were the times.

After the divorce, Barbara decided that she needed a different life and left El Paso for New England. David stayed back in the care of her mother so he could finish school, as she moved to the East Coast to work in marketing for the Pacific Bell Company—unheard of in the 1950s. She was basically a female *Mad Men* from the TV series for the phone company. Barbara would tell stories of being in the hot, arid desert of El Paso, Texas, to then having to climb over piles of snow in the middle of the street on her way to work in a frigid New England storm.

While she was in New England, she dated periodically but mostly focused on her work. In 1977, she was transferred to the Reno, Nevada, desert to help get the marketing department up and running for the West Coast office.

Living 20 miles outside the office and in a city lacking in public transportation, unlike New England, Barbara decided she needed to learn how to drive. She bought a brand-new orange GMC sedan, quite fashionable for the time. There was one small problem: Barbara didn't know how to drive. She enrolled in driving lessons, where she met the true love of her life, Peter, who soon moved in and lived with her until his death in the early 2000s. She never dated again.

I first met Barbara when I was 18 months old in 1979. When my parents moved to a suburb of Reno, they were greeted by our new neighbor, Barbara, and her partner, Peter. My parents would describe her at that time as achieved and successful, and when I say elegant and put together, that is an understatement. Barbara was the height of fashion and sophistication—truly cosmopolitan. She also had a deep love for cats.

Barbara and Peter were the neighborhood grandparents. They helped raise the children in our little area. With busy working parents, I was routinely at Barbara's house for most dinners, holidays, and weekends. My neighborhood friends were there, as well. We would play dress up with Barbara's amazing vintage 50s clothes, have dinner parties, learn female social graces, and play with the many, many cats she had rescued. My appreciation and love for the finer things, fancy cheeses, cats, and Paris all come from Barbara. Peter would teach us woodworking by building bike jumps, how to fish, play poker, and that elves lived in his beer. Barbara would take us to school if our parents forgot and to Macy's when each girl turned 14 to get proper skincare products and makeup—because a lady should always take care of herself.

Barbara always made sure we were fed, taken care of, and loved. I'm not completely feral because of her.

When I was 13, Barbara took me and another neighborhood kid, Amber (17), on a trip to France. Looking back at it now, what a freaking *saint* of a woman to take two teenage girls on *her* trip to France. She even took us to Euro Disney because we begged her since it had just opened. We toured Paris, attended mass at Notre-Dame, stayed in a country chateau where I rode horses with the count(!), and ate at the Michelin-starred Jules Verne in the Eiffel Tower and the La Tour d'Argent that was even featured on the famous TV show *Lifestyles of the Rich and Famous*.

Barbara did have a slight problem trying to drive a stick shift through the country, and ultimately, 13-year-old me drove the car back to the rental place to beg them for an automatic. I'm sure the clutch was totally shot in that Ford Fiesta! That was my first trip to Paris and France. I've had such a love for those places ever since.

Even after growing up and moving out of my parents' home next door to Barbara's, we all kept in touch with her. She was there for all the major events in my life: My high school graduation, my 21st birthday dinner, college graduation, law school graduation, my 30th birthday dinner, and my 40th. She has been there for the neighborhood kids' marriages, graduations, and births of their children, as well. Barbara was the parent or grandparent we all needed when our own weren't available or unable. She filled that gap. Sometimes, I wonder if that is because she felt guilty on some level for leaving her son David to be raised by her mother in Texas while she pursued her own life and dreams.

Barbara would tell me about her son David when I would call to check in with her. She told me that after finishing high school in Texas, David moved to San Francisco to attend college, got married, and had a son of his own. Although he was further away, he would periodically check in with her and visit occasionally. Barbara would tell me, "David called and told me he got a job working as an extra on a film; we can watch it when it comes out," or that her grandson "Jake is reading and playing soccer at his school." It seemed he was doing well and that she was proud of him and his life.

Amber kept in touch the most with Barbara after she got married and moved to Salt Lake City, where she became a flight attendant. She would call Barbara each week to check in and be sure to send her birthday and Christmas presents. I remained closer to Reno as my home base and could be more present for Barbara as she aged. I would call her from my travels around the world and check in with her to see if she needed anything.

As Barbara aged, she was progressively uncomfortable driving and needed a little more help. I would take her grocery shopping and to get kitty food. Around that time, David got divorced and became estranged from his ex-wife and son. He got into drugs and would call Barbara for money. Of course, she would send him cash or pay for his expenses. She would mention in passing that "David moved to LA and isn't doing well. He said it is tough down there to get into acting. So, I sent him some more money for his cat." I would inquire, "More money?" And she would sheepishly say that she sent him money for his cat's vet bills. Because "the poor kitty was sick again." Drug addicts know exactly which heartstrings to pull on to get what they want. David then moved to Reno and weaseled his way into her home since Peter had passed years prior. As a drug addict with a mental illness, he was volatile and verbally abusive. There is no way Peter would have put up with this nonsense and disrespect toward Barbara.

I remember the day Barbara called me and said, "You're not going to be happy." Then she told me David had moved in. From the moment he set foot in her house, he had been slowly destroying it as he siphoned her money. As a "resident" of her home, law enforcement had no way to remove him without a formal eviction and court order. He would tell me, "Good luck getting me out. I belong here now."

Addicts, scammers, and abusers know and use the law and scare tactics to remain in a property.

One day, when I came by to check on Barbara and take her to lunch and grocery shopping, she told me how abusive her son was and that she wanted to set up a will to be sure he couldn't have a say in her care and that he wouldn't receive anything after she passed.

She knew I did estate planning and wanted to get her affairs in order. Instead of a will, which would have to go through the probate process when she passed, we set up an estate plan and a revocable living trust. Barbara knew she needed to establish it while she was "young" enough and able to convey her financial and medical wishes and preserve all her hard work. We got all her paperwork in order, and she appointed me to be her power of attorney agent, meaning I could advocate for her wishes and get her son removed.

David did the favor for me. A few months later, in a drug-fueled episode, he tried to kill himself and, in the process, Barabara. High and delusional in her home, David started the car in the garage and opened the door to the house so it would fill with carbon monoxide in the middle of the night. Thankfully, Barbara had a carbon monoxide alarm in the house, which woke her up, and she called 911. They were both taken to the hospital, and Barbara was luckily okay.

I got a restraining order that day and served David in his hospital bed; at last, he had to leave her house. How he wasn't charged with attempted murder, I'll never know. The temporary restraining order was granted, and he had the audacity a month later to try to fight the extension of the order. He showed up to court attempting to get back into her home! The judge saw right through him and extended the order for a year. Because I had the power of attorney documents in place, this was an easy process.

Barbara continued to handle her own affairs into her early 90s, balancing her checking account to the penny. I would continue to come by and help her with basic cleaning, groceries, and her mail. One day, I noticed that she had forgotten to pay some bills and was overpaying others. At that point, she decided she didn't want to manage her affairs anymore and relinquished serving as a trustee for her estate plan and trust. I slowly started moving her finances over to online billing and bill pay. I could set up her accounts and make sure expenses were being paid on time. Barbara could still see everything and have a say in what was being done, and she continued to balance her checkbook to the penny, but now nothing was being missed.

Since the incident with David, Barbara hadn't slept much and became a little paranoid that he would show up at the house. She would routinely tell me when I saw her, "I heard a noise last night outside. I know David was out there." Or "I think David drove by the house last night. You don't think he can get in, do you? Do you think the kitties are safe? He wouldn't hurt the cats, right?"

It broke my heart that a 90-year-old woman who was so good to everyone around her should have to live in fear. I did what I could to assuage her fears and let her know she was safe. I installed motion cameras and had her home remodeled after the damage he had caused. She was not happy that we did not reinstall her grass and opted for a low-maintenance yard instead. Little 98-pound, now 91-year-old Barbara would tell me, "I will mow the lawn! I can do that just fine. I've always mowed the law, and if it is too much for you to do, I will do it." That used to make me laugh.

Due to building my estate planning business, I could work and travel the world while being present to help Barbara. I essentially became her caretaker as Amber lived farther away. Barbara would call me and say, "I have a problem," and I would drop everything and drive out to her house to fix whatever needed it. There is no way in this day and age that I would have been able to help her like I did if I had worked a 9-5 for someone else. With the care she needed for those "problems" and how often I was at her house, I would have been fired the first week.

Luckily, we had gotten her estate plan and revocable living trust in place years before, so when she started to decline, I could step in and handle her affairs for her. With the powers of attorney documents, I took care of her bills, made sure her house was in order, took her to the doctor, and advocated for her care. When the time came that she was struggling with even small day-to-day activities, I could arrange in-home care.

When Barbara turned 92, she began falling and was no longer able to stay safely in her home. It crushed me to take her from her home of 40 years and move her into a group home. When I would visit, she would ask me when we were going home. She only needed care for the last three months of her life, and during that time, she wasn't always sure who I was, but she did associate me with someone who handled business. Barbara would tell me to get back to work and go take care of the accounts.

> **We spend so much of our lives working that many people revert back to believing they are in their younger working lives when they decline. I think it is so important to do something you can enjoy because of this.**

When Barbara was ready to pass, Amber was able to come and spend a few days with her. Her former daughter-in-law and grandson had previously visited once before. Out of duty I had called them and said she was ready to go and asked if they wanted to come and say their goodbyes. They came, but only to inquire about items they wanted from her home and to be sure they got a copy of her death certificate, so they could get her death benefit.

> **What kind of person comes and spends less than 15 minutes with a dying loved one to then ask about a death certificate when they haven't even passed yet?! These are the types of people estate planning protects against.**

When Barbara peacefully passed on May 7, 2022, I was able to grieve her loss. I didn't have to scramble to file a probate petition with the court to fight her drug-addict son, former daughter-in-law, and grandson. I didn't have to send out notices of her passing to alert these predators or have her passing published in the newspaper. Her affairs were kept private, as she wished.

I was also able to take care of all the necessary tasks for her right away. I didn't have to wait. The court didn't need to approve my actions. I didn't have to cover expenses and wait for reimbursement or hire an attorney to ensure they were handling the to-dos the right way and in a timely fashion.

Barbara and her affairs were addressed immediately and with care. This was only possible through her estate plan. As I wasn't technically related to her, without those documents, my hands would have been tied. And without any reliable family members to help her when she was declining, she, more than likely, would have become a ward of the state. The thought of that still makes me sick to my stomach.

I share Barbara's story to impart the importance of getting these things in order. How easy (paperwork-wise) it was to handle all her affairs and make sure she was safe and taken care of. How reassuring that no random "family" could come in and take what wasn't theirs and/or what she would not have wanted them to have. I could fulfill *her* wishes, not those of the state or anyone else.

What would have happened if Barbara didn't have her estate plan in place? Would I still be going through the probate process today? Would I be fighting her drug-addict son who tried to kill her and her estranged family members who only came out of the woodwork to get something? These people never bothered to check in on her or cared about her when she was alive but expected to be given her life's work when she was gone?

This is why I am so passionate about estate planning. I want to make these basic legal services more accessible to everyone and widely disseminate to the everyday person the information and resources I had access to through law school. I want everyone to have the tools to create an affordable estate plan without having to trudge down to a stuffy lawyer's office, feel intimated, be talked down to, and have to spend thousands of dollars for it. These services and legal vehicles should be accessible and affordable for everyone.

The average probate costs about $28,000. That's just the midrange. Most costs are typically much higher than that. That is money that could have gone to your children, charity, or pets for their care. That's generational wealth that can be preserved by a small amount of pre-planning on your part.

> **Whether you are in my situation or just want to be sure your loved ones don't have to go through the nightmare of probate, it's now easier and more affordable than ever to get your estate plan in place.**

Check out my website, www.yourestateplan.online, where I have a ton of tools, resources, and education, so you can feel empowered to protect yourself and those you love. I also share tons of educational resources on my social media pages, podcast, and YouTube channel.

So that's the story of an amazing woman, Barbara. What will your story be?

About the Author

Lindsay Wheeler is a native Nevadan who obtained her bachelor's degree at the University of Nevada, Reno, in the field of international business. In 2007, Ms. Wheeler obtained her Juris Doctorate at Lincoln Law School in Sacramento before returning to the Reno/Tahoe area. She went on to obtain her MBA in 2018.

Ms. Wheeler was a judicial law clerk for the late Honorable Judge Robert H. Perry at the Washoe County Second Judicial District Court for two years and worked as an extern with Nevada Supreme Court Justice Michael Cherry. Ms. Wheeler has also worked at the Nevada State Legislature as a Senate Judiciary Committee secretary for the 2013 Legislative Session.

Ms. Wheeler has worked in the legal field for more than 20 years and started Your Estate Plan online to provide people with an alternative way to complete their estate plan and navigate the legal process for themselves instead of hiring a lawyer with costly fees.

In her spare time, Ms. Wheeler enjoys traveling the world, a nice glass of wine, and experiencing the outdoors.

CHAPTER 5

The Equitable Distribution of Parenting: Redefining the Default Parent

Michele Kelber

"In the earlier stages of feminism, women were told they could not be whatever it was they wanted to be. After women became those things anyway, then society said, 'All right, you're now a lawyer or a mechanic or an astronaut— but that's only OK if you continue to do the work you did before—if you take care of the children, cook three meals a day, and are multi-orgasmic until dawn."
—Gloria Steinem

A friend once said to me, "The women's lib movement is a disservice to women." She went on to explain how, although it allowed us to enter the workforce, it did nothing about mitigating the amount of work women do at home or the emotional weight of parenting carried by women.

Now, just to be clear, the conversation continued, and I contributed my two cents that The Women's Liberation Movement did magic for women like me: Single, business owner, homeowner, credit card possessor, credit-rating-having, birth-control-using, independent human. Without it, I wouldn't have been able to create this life that I love so dearly. Without it, many women, our predecessors, seemingly went to college just to get their MRS. degree, not to pursue their passions and dreams because that truly was their only option.

So, the Women's Liberation Movement is a win in some ways and a very long work in progress in others. Don't get me started on equal pay and career advancement after pregnancy.

The reality is that in most households, parenting or co-parenting as we call it now is not divided evenly, with moms shouldering more of the responsibilities of maintaining the house, as well as the emotional weight of parenting, as she often looks at the future and meeting everyone's needs. Mom continues to be the default parent outside the home, as schools and society literally contact her or defer to only her in matters about the children.

Women who work outside the home walk through the door every night and sometimes on the weekends to another unpaid 40+ hour-a-week job. They are expected to perform exceptionally in a short amount of time and are often undervalued and unappreciated. I highly doubt the intention of the Women's Movement was to double our workload. Yet, it came with no instructions on how to create equity and new roles for both parents, only the freedom for a woman to get a job outside the home, where, frankly, a lot of women are underpaid, undervalued, and unappreciated. Don't worry; the performance expectations are higher than average, though!

Now, I don't have the answers, but I have some ideas. I am a champion for women and children. My goal is for each to know their voice and enable themselves to live the lives they love. Who I am at my core is equity and love.

To write this chapter, I took the time to talk to different parents: single by choice, widowed, gay, lesbian, divorced, heterosexual, and a few stay-at-home dads, but this book is for women. Not a mom? Not a woman? Working in the home? Working out of the home? Not sure if you want to be a mom or work outside the home? Whatever it is, keep reading. You will find yourself here.[4*]

What This Chapter Is and Isn't

This chapter is meant to raise families up, however that family looks. It is not intended to tear down men or women or isolate people. It's an opportunity for me to share what I've seen over the years: moms steering the ship, dads not in the loop, trends in parenting, challenges in communication style, theories I've tested, and thoughts I have for the future through the research I've done on equity in parenting. I'm not a scientist, so take it all with a grain of salt, and try it on. You never know what's a good fit.

---

4 * My use of the terms "men" and "women" is based on findings but can easily be adjusted to include partners of any gender with similar personalities.

In my research and through my experiences, I discovered three key factors that impact parenting and partnership more than we realize:

- Women and men are inherently different, and two moms may be better than one.
- Kids bond with people who spend time with them.
- The default parent IS the mom.

Women and Men are Inherently Different; Two Moms May Be Better Than One

There is a book about Venus and Mars. The content centers on the fact that although men and women are part of the same species, in most cases, we, women, and they, men, are wildly different. This includes our self-expression, our expectations of ourselves and others, what is important to us, and generally how we see the world. Our intentions don't always match up, and the parenting dance can seem like a series of foibles with feet being stomped on left and right by our partner.

Despite these differences, at our core, as parents, we love.

To make a sustainable difference for our children and co-parent and create a home and society of partnership, we must acknowledge that we, as varying genders, live life through different lenses and scopes.

Two ways to break down our barriers with our co-parent are to consider how they see and interact in the world. A great practice I've adopted in business and life is knowing a person's love language and personality tendency. You can read more about the importance and nuances of each in Chapter 3 of my book, "Where Kids Are," in *How Not to Ruin Your Kids: A Practical Guide to Raising Happy, Independent, Equipped Children*.

Knowing a person's love language and personality tendency allows you a little insight into how they express and receive love as well as what drives them in life (whether themselves, others, a need to know, or not much). Understanding these basics profoundly impacts our ability to communicate and relate to one another. Both are great tools for understanding your children, too.

If your co-parent feels warm and fuzzy when you verbally share your appreciation, but you focus on showing your thanks by spending time with them, they may not fully experience the love you have for them.

If your partner needs to know why something needs to be done and you don't tell them, their personality trait won't allow them to understand the importance of the task, and they probably won't do it. It's worth the time to investigate their communication style and yours!

Agree or not, oftentimes, men do things because they want to; their choice solves a problem at that moment, and whatever it is is important to them personally. Women do things because they know they need to get done, their choice factors in the impact on the future, and their actions are for everyone.

A great example is when my mom would tell us no when we kids asked for a late-night soda or popsicle or a whodunit mystery on TV. It's not that she wasn't any fun; she just knew giving in to those wants would've resulted in my brother and me being up all night, bouncing off the walls from sugar, or being too scared to fall asleep or stay asleep without night terrors! And that meant tomorrow's trip to the beach almost certainly would be traumatic for everyone. The car might've actually had to be turned around.

My dad may have said yes because in the moment we were badgering him (problem solved), he couldn't foresee the consequences (nothing would happen in that instant other than glee), and he wanted to make us happy.

The point is that our focus as women and our desires may not even be what is on our partner's radar. A lot of men don't care about beds being made, dishes in the sink, or kids being bathed each night. Yes, a gross generalization, I know.

When something isn't on our radar, women or men, it is not going to get done unless someone asks us to do it. Read that again.

Invisible Labor

I spoke with a household of two moms. What I found astounding from the conversation is that when one isn't available, the other picks up the slack of household chores and contributes to the functionality of the home *without a conversation or having to be asked.*

In light of this, I checked in with a female friend who is married to a man. She grouses sometimes that her husband will do tasks if she asks but is mystified that he can't figure out what needs to be done on his own. Maybe it's because he considers certain chores and jobs hers, or maybe he thinks she enjoys doing them (I've heard reasoning: "I thought you did that because *you like to.*"). Regardless, men and women lack the symbioses that seem to exist in a two-mom household. Women, my friends, *do all the things.* We do them because they need to get done, and we know how essential they are to our lives and well-being in the future. We do them because we love our families, and we need some semblance of order in our lives. We do them because it's the way it's always been. However, we would not turn down an assist on the field!

Kids Bond with People Who Spend Time with Them

My dad was a child psychologist. One day, when he was years past retirement in his mid-80s, I was talking to him about something I was teaching my nephew. I was so lit up, almost boasting about the experience. My dad jumped in and said, "Michele, spending time with a child isn't about what you teach them; it's about spending time with them, so they know they are important to you and the world."

In that moment you could probably see the lightbulb appear over my head.

We all try so hard to create amazing experiences for our kids when, in reality, they want our time and connection. This can happen when doing anything! How do you feel as an adult when someone gives you undivided attention? Pretty great.

There have been so many studies investigating whether children are better off parented by biological parents, a mother and a father, heterosexual couples, or LGBTQ+ parents. The agreement now is that it doesn't make much difference.[5]

What seems to be more important is that consistency, love, boundaries, and time spent with a child is what enables them to grow and flourish. It is irrelevant who their parent is, the gender they identify as, how many parents there are, and if there is a biological tie. It's how you show up that makes a difference.

The Default Parent Is the Mom

Regardless of the studies on bonding, the default parent to the outside world is always the mom. I talked to two stay-at-home dads during my interviews. Both told stories of how inevitably the school nurse would call the mom and not the stay-at-home dad. We speculated that maybe it was because the mom filled out the form and her name was first, or it is the go-to for most administrators.

---

5 "Children of Same-Sex Couples Fare at Least as Well as in Other Families – Study." The Guardian, March 6, 2023. https://www.theguardian.com/science/2023/mar/06/children-of-same-sex-couples-fare-at-least-as-well-as-in-other-families-study.

In both cases, even after gentle reminders, the elementary school continued to call the mom at her job rather than the dad at his job as a *stay-at-home dad*! When the kids entered middle school and high school, the tables turned a bit, and the dads started getting called. It could be that the child spoke up, and their instructions were trusted at that age, or the school caught on and entered the modern times.

RBG Blazed a Parenting Path

Dinners with Ruth by Nina Totenberg and an interview with Joan Williams by Michel Martin on NPR's *All Things Considered* both recount the default parenting dilemma Ruth Bader Ginsberg faced over balancing motherhood and work.

While a professor at Columbia Law School, RBG got yet another call about her spirited child from the head of the school, insisting she come down at once to hear what was going on. Having stayed up all night writing a brief, Ginsberg stated, "This child has two parents. Please alternate calls. And it's his father's turn."

After that, the calls to RBG were fewer and fewer. Initially, the school put time and consideration into whether they should bother the child's father at work but did not offer the same consideration to the mother. When they were essentially cut off by the mother, they dealt with the challenges on their own. So, all you working moms out there. It's not you. It's them.

Now, I think there is a time and a place to share incidences and information with parents, but the time and the place for non-emergencies is after working hours, after school, or nowadays, in an email. We do not need to call parents for a hangnail.

So, Now What?

Let's accept, first of all, that things aren't going to change unless *we* do something. As much as we would like our partners and the world to anticipate our needs and meet us where we are, we may be waiting a long time. Remember, men and women are very different, and society hasn't quite figured out that men are as capable of raising children and handling problems as women.

As Brené Brown says, "Clear is Kind." Set up your family, schools, and activities with plans that support your family dynamic.

Communicate Your Needs to Your Partner and the World

Because men and women are so different, people in heterosexual relationships may need to communicate more, unlike the symbiosis of a two-mom house. If this is your dynamic, share with your partner what your needs are and what you could use some help with at home. It doesn't have to be significant or emotional, just "Laundry needs to get done, and I can't do that and make dinner." Equitably split the household responsibilities. Make a freakin' chore chart if you need to so that things get done around the house. When it comes to housework, don't forget about the kids! They can do things at any age. See Chapter 6: "Responsibility," in *How Not to Ruin Your Kids,* for more information about chores and their benefits to kids. Here's another tip: If you have extra income, outsource tasks that neither one of you wants to do.

This also applies to rewiring the world to support a new default parent. Let the schools and activities know who to call first. Channel RBG, and stick to your boundaries. If they do call you, and you can't help answering, ask if it's an emergency, then say, "Please call their father." *Don't make the call to your co-pare*nt; let the school handle it. I get there is a concern if it is an emergency. If it is, and you are not reachable for whatever reason, they will call the next contact.

Let Go of Mom Guilt—Spend Quality Time with Your Kids

As a mom working outside the home, you are setting an example for your children that women are valued, intelligent, driven, and contribute to the world and the family. If your partner is staying home caring for your children full-time, it's okay. They can do it just as well as you. If your child is in daycare, that's okay, too! To be honest, sometimes it's better that moms work outside the home. Not everyone has the financial luxury of having a parent stay home, and in many cases, parenting young children is not a match for every adult. I'd be bored and frustrated at all times, for instance. Allow yourself the grace to recognize your strengths, and do what's best for your family.

> **Remember, kids enjoy being with you, not necessarily what you do together. So, have them help you make dinner or wash the car if that's what needs to happen. Just be with them.**

And lastly, moms, you are doing a great job. Take it in. Know that you love fiercely and are loved back just as much, if not more. We appreciate you. We love you, and we believe in you.

You can learn more about Michele and schedule a free discovery call at gantrykids.com/consulting-information.

About the Author

Michele Kelber is the author of *How Not to Ruin Your Kids: A Practical Guide to Raising Happy, Independent, Equipped Children*. She is also the founder & owner of Gantry Kids & Teens, an independent kids gym in NYC providing programs to school-age children. Through fitness, Michele's philosophies provide a supportive, organic environment that is "Building Tomorrow's Leaders Today" while fostering critical learning. She fights fiercely to allow kids to be kids, advocating for unstructured play, outdoor time, physical activity, and personal agency. Her book is a culmination of her decades-long career working with children and families and her love letter to the world.

Michele earned a BA in Fine Arts, with a Spanish minor, then a JD and an MBA. Coupled with a long-standing career working with children, Michele maintains her license to practice law in

New York, which has proven helpful as a business owner and legal counsel to other aspiring entrepreneurs. In addition to her academic achievements, she is a certified health coach and holds multiple certificates in fitness specific to coaching kids.

As Michele's passion is human connection and building relationships, she is committed to the growth and development of children as well as their parents and caregivers and does so through consulting, workshops, and mentoring for adults. Michele's goal is to enable children to know and use their voice in the world, contribute no matter their age, and be independent.

Her love language is quality time, and she spends much of it with her friends and family, building lasting memories, traveling, and hiking with her 15-year-old dog Luna.

Michele lives in Colorado but will always have an East Coast attitude and love for NYC.

CHAPTER 6

How to Eat a Financial Sandwich

Caroline Tanis

"Money is only a tool. It will take you wherever you wish,
but it will not replace you as the driver."
—Ayn Rand

L et me set a likely scene: You wake up at 5:00 a.m. every weekday, hoping for a few minutes of silence before the rest of your household comes barreling down the stairs full of energy you wish you had. After squeezing in a quick workout, you and your spouse juggle getting the kids ready and off to school before you both fly out the door to make it in time for your morning work meetings.

As you sit in the 48th-floor conference room overlooking the city skyline, your mind wanders to all the bills piling up at home. Summer camp tuition is due next week for your two children; your parents' at-home nurse is asking for a raise, and don't forget you need a new car this year. To top it off, your in-laws have been begging you to spend the kids' spring break at their new place in

Florida, which will require plane tickets to be purchased during one of the most expensive weeks of the year. Scribbling down the cost of each item on the side of your notepad makes your head ache.

You ask yourself, *when did life get so expensive?* and *how did we end up being the financial caretakers for so many people?*

What the Heck Is the Sandwich Generation?

The term "sandwich generation," simply put, means a group of Gen Xers and Millennials that have found themselves raising their own children while simultaneously taking care of aging parents.

> **But why does this feel like such uncharted territory? Well, it is.**

The CDC cites the average life expectancy for men is 74.8 years and 80.2 years for females.[6] Rewind to a century ago when males were expected to live around 53.6 years and females 78.93 years.[7] Most people were lucky to even see their retirement years, and as women, we often weren't tasked with working and taking care of children and our parents.

This sandwich generation was introduced to us in the classic movie *Charlie and the Chocolate Factory.* Your life may feel like

6 "FastStats - Life Expectancy." Centers for Disease Control and Prevention, May 2, 2024. https://www.cdc.gov/nchs/fastats/life-expectancy.htm.

7 Tennant, Amie. "What Was It Like 100 Years Ago Today?" Family Search, March 31, 2020. https://www.familysearch.org/en/blog/100-years-ago-today-1920.

the beginning at-home scenes of that film. Charlie's mom has to not only raise her son but take care of her and her husband's parents all crammed into that one bed. Plus, she is maintaining a home on a tight budget. Imagine if, in addition, she was working to grow her career or business . . . which brings us to the modern day and present you.

Maybe You Love Sandwiches?

Being stretched in two directions might be the life you've always dreamed of. Marriage to a supportive spouse, raising healthy, beautiful children while still having your parents around, and striving to live life to the fullest, that's all well and good, but we can also be incredibly thankful for our lives while wanting to make changes for the better. The two ideas are not mutually exclusive.

So, how do we handle being financially sandwiched?

During this season of your life, you are trying to monetarily support young children, save for retirement and other dreams, and balance the cost of aging parents and in-laws who could be located in different corners of the country.

The first step toward managing the squeeze is communication. I encourage you to read through this entire chapter to learn about what I've found works best in financial planning before jumping up to talk to your loved ones about your and their current financial situations.

You might roll your eyes at this suggestion because it feels obvious. If your first thought was, *of course, we need to talk about the different activities, problems, and costs in our lives,* I hear you. Honestly, I've been you and still have moments where I slip back into that old way of thinking. And although we know that this is the first logical step in creating more ease around building your dream life, talking about what you need and what's stretching you beyond your comfort zone is often the easiest thing to skip. We know we need to talk about the sandwich in the room, but it makes us uneasy, so we push it off, and it winds up on the to-do list with no real timeline—until there is. But by then, it's probably too late, and we're in the midst of an emergency.

Additionally, we assume that the other person or people in our lives know what we're thinking. *How could your mother-in-law not know how difficult it is to get the whole family to Florida during a hectic travel time?* Well, in her eyes, all she and your father-in-law can think about is how amazing it would be to have all their family under their new roof and show off the people they love most around town.

Everyone has their own expectations around what they expect other people to do in their lives, whether emotional, physical, or even financial. To rise up and become our truest selves, we need to take charge of communicating all these needs. It begins with talking to ourselves. No, I don't necessarily mean a formal sit-down conversation with yourself. You might take a walk, journal, or meditate on what the future can look like.

Start Talking

We will next focus on communicating your financial needs, thoughts, wants, and questions to the different people in your life, but you may find that this process merges with other thoughts in your mind. That's normal.

And that's because money is emotional. We all have a money story or a history with money.

It has to do with how we grew up hearing our parents talk about money, our socioeconomic status, different economic events that happened during our most formative years, and so many tiny factors that impacted us at the time—although we may not have realized it.

I share this with you because you likely have different feelings around finances than others participating in these conversations. We can't force someone to change how they feel about a particular topic, but we do need to understand and be prepared that our partner, children, friend, or family member will react based on their own money story.

The Process

Here's the order of communication to achieve your most optimal life-changing outcome:

**Yourself → Your Spouse → Your Children →
Your Parents or other people in your life for
who you are financially responsible**

Let's break this down and explore each person's role and potential expectations/thoughts.

Yourself: Before you can converse with anyone else, you need to understand how *you feel* about your current financial situation and responsibilities. This may even mean taking a step back and writing down all your current financial responsibilities and what you project them to be. I encourage you to be honest about what you will have to take on (or have already taken on).

I did this exercise, and between running my business, having big, audacious dreams, and accepting that I am the only child of divorced parents living in two different states, I found myself being pulled in so many different directions physically, financially, and emotionally. And this wasn't even the detailed list of all the small things that can sneak up on us (remember summer camp? Braces? All those birthday parties?). Someone has to manage and pay for them.

Before I went down the rabbit hole of adding up every little financial responsibility, I stopped to ask myself two distinct questions:

1. Who *can* I be financially responsible for?
2. Who do I *want* to be financially responsible for?

Make sure you get clear on these questions before having conversations with anyone.

As women, we are so quick to take care of everyone else and their emotional, physical, and financial needs. But we can't continue caring for others if it means forgoing our dreams. So, answer those questions!

Also, know it's inevitable, over time, that your financial situation will change. As you and your spouse's careers grow, you may start to make more money, an inheritance might fall into your lap, or you could have less financial responsibility in an area of your life. As these shifts occur, you can add more items from the "want" category to the "can" category.

For example, one of my clients received an inheritance that was more money than she ever imagined having. But she wanted to make sure she was honoring her father's legacy and values, so we went to her "want category" and talked about which line item made the most sense to check off. After conversations around what she could use the money for and what felt in alignment, my client decided to use a majority of the funds to fully support her children through college. She also donated a percentage to a charity supporting families caring for loved ones with her father's illness.

Your Spouse or Partner: No matter if you are married, living with a partner, or share financial responsibilities with someone else, this section will apply to you. Please note that I will use "partner" and "spouse" interchangeably throughout.

We all have different relationships with our spouses and finances. And as I mentioned before, we all have our own money stories. You may be open and willing to talk about your finances with your partner, and they may want to avoid it any way they can or vice versa. Regardless of where you stand, these tips that I share with clients about having financial conversations together will start the two of you off on the right foot and keep you there:

- **Make it fun**. Plan a date night, go somewhere neutral, and open your favorite bottle of wine. Conversations around money don't have to be stressful, painful, or uncomfortable. But many of us grew up in households where talking about money was taboo, or we learned from society, "It isn't polite to talk about money." I don't subscribe to this. I *love* to talk about money because it is a tool and resource that gets us closer to living our dream life. You have my full permission to do the same.
- **Let your partner know ahead of time that you want to talk about finances and the future**. Resist springing it on them.

  - Use open communication, and help set the tone. Just as you don't want to be judged and attacked for your money choices, you need to treat your spouse the same way.
  - Be open to using a moderator. When working with clients, I often assign them homework to do individually, and then we come back a week later, and I work to moderate conversations around finances. I'm a neutral third party looking to build a plan rather than judging their choices.

During this conversation, compare your answers regarding who you can be financially responsible for versus who you want to be financially responsible for. For instance, you may decide you can support the kids going to college but don't want to pay for everything, so they also have some financial responsibility. Or that you want to help your parents by physically allowing them to live with you, but they will need to be financially responsible for their medical care and assistance.

Your Children: This conversation will differ for every parent, depending on their children's age(s). For college-age and under, get clear and communicate what you can afford for schooling and support during their college years. This topic usually comes up during the middle-high school years because, as we know, any earlier than that can be hard for children to understand, especially when it comes to timelines that pertain to them in the distant future. As college conversations begin, ensure you and your spouse (or co-parent) are on the same page about what you can and want to afford for schooling.

If you have adult children, communicate your intended financial support for their major life events. Remember, there is no wrong or right answer here. Everyone has individual thoughts and feelings about paying for events like weddings, housing, grandchildren, going to college, etc. The important part is clearly communicating your intentions to your children so that they can plan their financial futures.

Your Parents and In-Laws: Watching our parents age is difficult, and so is the dynamic as we shift from our parents taking care of us to them needing care. This transition can be more natural in some parent-child relationships, but many find that shift hard. Perhaps your parents need more support around the house or increased medical care. As we are living longer, they may require someone to help them more frequently and for longer periods.

Communication around your parents' and in-laws' concerns isn't an easy topic to address. But it's one I feel overly passionate about.

Why?

Time and time again, I have seen this responsibility fall to the daughter in a family versus their male sibling(s). As women, we are the default caretakers for our aging parents during our highest working years. The Family Caregiver Alliance found that "The cost impact of caregiving on the individual female caregiver in terms of lost wages and Social Security benefits equals $324,044."[8] This could be the difference between paying for your children's college, a huge down payment on a second home, or the ability to retire when and where you want.

The first step in fixing this problem is openly communicating with our parents and in-laws about what they can physically and financially expect from us as caregivers. Keep in mind that you

---

8 By the National Center on Caregiving at Family Caregiver Alliance and was reviewed by Phyllis Mutschler, Ph.D. "Women and Caregiving: Facts and Figures." Women and Caregiving: Facts and Figures - Family Caregiver Alliance. Accessed August 20, 2024. https://www.caregiver.org/resource/women-and-caregiving-facts-and-figures/.

also need to be clear with them on *how* you will afford and exert your time, money, and other resources to support them. When you follow this communication plan in the order I am laying out, you and your spouse will know what you can and want to offer for support.

Like your discussion with your partner, go into this conversation with an open mind. I also suggest clients schedule a family meeting beforehand, so all parties can plan what they want to discuss rather than being blindsided.

The key to a successful conversation with aging parents is to have it before it's too late.

Pre-pandemic, we lost my great aunt. Watching her deteriorate so quickly was the catalyst our family needed to begin our planning.

Keep at It . . .

You've done the hard part, but we still have a little more work to do! I struggle to celebrate the small wins, and you might feel the same. If so, I want you to pause and take a moment to appreciate how far you've come. Whether you've held yourself accountable to reading this far or already had some of these conversations with your family members, you have made a step(s) toward building your dream life.

Now, I encourage you to keep reading and take another step toward making that dream a reality.

Next Steps: Start. I know it sounds silly, but the hardest part of changing your financial future is taking the first step. Begin by asking yourself questions around who you can be and who you want to be financially responsible for. Know that your answers to these questions will change as time goes on and life evolves.

After having this conversation with yourself and your family members, it's time to create a plan that maps out your timeline and financial responsibility for big life events. Whether you design this with a financial professional like me or on your own is totally up to you and your comfort level. It's most essential to create a plan you can revisit not only throughout the year but in the years to come.

Even if you work with a professional, understand the largest chunk of work goes into creating the financial plan.

Your advisor can't read your mind, so expect a high level of communication between sharing your goals and your current financial situation. A financial planner should then have (at least) an annual check-in with you and your spouse to review your goals, determine if they are still relevant, and see how you are progressing in making your dreams a reality. Your financial advisor should also work to help you create actionable steps on the goals you are still pursuing.

Keep in mind that those cans and wants we spoke about before will change. Heck, that's what keeps life fun and interesting! You may find that after a recent promotion and consultation about your financial plan, you can increase contributions to your children's college savings accounts and still take that dream vacation.

The key to thriving while financially sandwiched is to keep having conversations with your loved ones throughout the years so everyone knows what is expected of them and what they can expect of others. Without this step, your plan and, more importantly, making your dream life a reality will be challenging.

Go for It!

Know that you are worthy of having this dream life. As we perform life's daily tasks, adding more to our to-do list through conversations and planning can be daunting. But you must understand that part of achieving that dream life is rising up and finding out who you truly are. Let each chapter of this book help you discover your truth. They were written just for you to help you *rise & find* yourself at the highest level possible in multiple areas of your life.

Your dream life will change and evolve with every discovery you make about your financial future. But it will become more beautiful than you can imagine if you let it.

Download a copy of the Women's Wealth Playbook to help you continue building your wealthiest dream life at www.tanis-fingroup.com.

About the Author

Caroline Tanis, CDFA®, is a financial advisor and strategist who focuses on helping her clients build their desired lifestyle. She works primarily with highly ambitious women and their families to create a financial plan. Caroline helps her clients determine their goals and future lifestyle to build plans specific to them.

Utilizing estate, retirement, trust, investment planning, and more, Caroline bridges the gap between where clients are now and where they want to go.

Caroline received her B.S. in Wealth Management and Financial Planning from the University of Delaware and her MBA in Finance from Saint Joseph's University.

She resides in New Jersey but is an avid traveler and always looking for her next destination. In addition, she is a proud dog mom to a dachshund, Chester, who loves to taste test for her while she is cooking.

CHAPTER 7

Regain Your Body's Wisdom

Brianna Frost-Smith

*"The greatest medicine of all is to teach people
how not to need it."*
—Hippocrates

Have you ever felt like you simply can't keep up with life? The pressure of getting everything done throughout the day and being present for your family these days can feel so overwhelming.

When it comes to caring for everyone else, women have been carrying the load on their shoulders for many years. But times are changing, and the time is now to put yourself first. Without you, that extensive list of to-dos would never be accomplished, it's impossible if your body is not functioning at its highest potential.

But how do you accomplish that?

Imagine a health program tailored to your unique needs, with every decision directed toward your body's wisdom. The secret to optimal health is not just about what you eat but understanding how your body responds to it. Nutrition response testing is the ultimate personal guide that will help transform your life so you can tackle any task. "Mom burn-out," while common and accepted as normal is, in fact, not.

Our bodies are under so much stress from the toxins of today's world that we cannot function at our highest potential.

I'm sure you've gone to the doctor for a blood work panel. Personally, this is where my journey to find an answer all started.

I was so exhausted every day that no matter how much sleep I got, I hit my breaking point. I had also struggled with eczema and constipation since I was a teenager.

After having every panel drawn you could think of and receiving the phone call from my doctor that everything "looks normal," I was not going to settle for that answer. Deep down, I knew something was wrong. Yes, I could have brushed it off and chalked it up to the fact that I was a new mom and life was different, but I was in my late twenties—too young to feel this type of exhaustion.

So, I did something about it.

When conventional medicine fell short of addressing my concerns, I searched around for an answer. Through a conversation with my dearest friend, I stumbled upon a recommendation to try nutrition response testing.

Like most people, I had never heard of this method before. But I was on a quest for holistic wellness, and this option stood out the most.

What I discovered was amazing! Nutrition Response Testing®, as taught in my advanced certified course, is a personalized road map to vitality shaped by your body's needs and signals. After receiving my results back and a few short weeks of being on a personalized program, I went from feeling like a zombie mom to my true age again. After experiencing my results, I knew I needed to help others and spread the word, so I embarked on my journey to become a certified Nutrition Response Testing® practitioner.

The Pivot

COVID had just begun when I was pregnant with my daughter. The rug had been ripped out from under the world, and everything was in shambles. I was in school working toward my RN but quickly changed my path as I watched everything unfold. The hospital rules got so intense during this time that my husband was not going to be allowed in the room during my labor and delivery. We changed our birth plan immediately once we heard that was the policy.

I had called all over New Jersey earlier that day to see if any available midwives could travel to our home. Luckily, I had learned about an amazing group of midwives in Pennington, New Jersey, who made a special exception for me as we were outside their travel zone. I think they could hear the desperation in my voice. These ladies were truly a Godsend. This was the year that the holistic world really impacted our life.

An Unwelcome Visitor

A few years into my practice, panic hit home.

Our daughter was diagnosed with Lyme disease, and our pediatrician only recommended antibiotics. Since we didn't agree with that, we chose a holistic route first.

Let me tell you, we are so glad we did!

If I had not taken that unknown leap into my career, we would have never been able to help my daughter gain her health back like she did. I had muscle tested her prior to receiving her blood work results that week, and sure enough, her results lined up with my muscle testing results. To keep a distance from my emotions and ensure our girl received the absolute best protocol, we decided it would be best to use another practitioner.

The pushback I received from family and friends was the hardest part for our family. "Why would you not want to go the traditional route, just give her the antibiotics?" I knew this was not the only way.

How did this all unfold right before our eyes?

Innocently enough, we had moved our daughter into her new big-girl room in August, next to our hallway closet holding the outdoor shower piping. A slow leak happened over time, of which we were unaware. Once we had the house tested for mold, we figured out where the leak was and went right to the source of the mold.

This leak had been creating Stachybotrys, also known as "black mold," one of the top ten dangerous molds you can encounter. Our daughter's bed was along the other side of that wall in her bedroom.

Although this mold growth was only the size of a baseball, it affected her health. Her inflammation started at the end of September, shortly after we moved her into that bedroom.

While our family was out of the house for over a month-and-a-half remediating, our daughter was on a strict detox protocol to remove unwanted pests in her system. Yes, "pests" plural. Prior to discovering the mold, we found out she had contracted Lyme disease, which can be transmitted not only by ticks but mosquitos, fleas, and even in utero. She never had a bullseye rash—a telltale sign—and her Lyme is considered chronic. She is doing amazing now and no longer testing for Lyme or mold. We had no idea this parasite was in her little body until she started to show symptoms. Her blood work tested positive when she was just three years old. Our bodies truly are amazing when it comes to healing themselves. Hers is certainly proving this to be the case.

Lyme is a Copycat

Lyme disease is wicked smart, which is why it is called "the great mimicker." Many even live with chronic Lyme without realizing they have it. Often, when antibiotics are introduced into the system, Lyme will hide deep in the tissues. It can disguise itself and change form quickly, making it hard for the body to detox and remove it.

> **Did you know that many who have taken the full dose of antibiotics for Lyme tend to have more symptoms later down the road that all lead back to Lyme? That's not always an effective treatment. Another reason I do what I do!**

As a side note: if you ever suspect mold in conjunction with Lyme disease, you need to address the mold first, or you will spin your wheels when it's time to detox.

The History of the Integrated Approach

Nutrition response testing has been around for many years as a unique form of applied kinesiology, known as "muscle testing," that can also be applied virtually. Long-distance testing based on Quantum Physics essentially means that everything is energetically tied together, which sets off a frequency. Both techniques offer an integrated approach to uncovering the root causes behind various issues.

In our practice, when the body's nervous system is tested, we receive an analysis, allowing us to determine which organs are not functioning as optimally as we would like. Analyses of different body surface areas indicate each organ's function and energy flow.

We receive this information through energy analysis. It's so amazing that everything on this planet gives off energy.

Once we determine which organs need attention we place a whole food supplement on the body that will address the stressed organ. If the body agrees with the supplement, meaning it is not stressing the organ, a locked muscle will result. We know then that this supplement will work for this particular organ or concern.

When we muscle test either virtually or in person, the signals we receive during the assessment determine the stressed organs and which organ we need to prioritize first. When light pressure is applied to a limb, such as an arm, and the limb weakens, it's an indicator that the organ we are testing is stressed. This response can happen if the body is dealing with a stressor, such as chemicals, metals, food, or immune challenges. Sometimes, we just need to simply add organ support to see an improvement.

Causes

Many causes might make someone sick. Our environment is rife with environmental stressors that can negatively affect our bodies. That's just one factor.

There are six common barriers to healing that a certified Nutrition Response Testing® practitioner identifies and targets during an assessment. These stressors are immune challenges, metal toxicities, food sensitivities, chemical toxicities, post-pandemic factors, and even scars.

Many adults suffer from hormone imbalances in today's world caused by many factors. How often have you sprayed or rubbed scented perfume directly on your thyroid? If you read the ingredients and realize you are applying these chemicals directly to the area that helps regulate your hormones, you might start putting the puzzle together. Unfortunately, every day, we are bombarded by innumerable chemicals. Certain chemicals are simply unavoidable. The human body is amazing and can filter out many things, but it might need assistance.

What Happens When You Are Chronically Ill

When stressors impact the nervous system, the brain's communication channels are disrupted, deteriorating our natural healing ability. Then, the body ceases to function at full capacity and begins to malfunction. As these malfunctions increase, the body becomes increasingly unbalanced, eventually leading to a state of dis-ease. Symptoms then show up as your body tries to cope with environmental stressors; this is the body's cry for assistance.

Symptoms do not happen overnight. Years of cumulative tissue damage must occur before they present. By that time, at least 70% of damage to affected tissues has occurred, indicating the presence of a malfunction, disease, or tissue damage. Sometimes, symptoms do not pinpoint the exact location or underlying cause(s). This is another reason we don't rely on symptoms for our answers. We don't guess; we test.

What You Can Do to Feel Better

Toxicity build-up is why ensuring our drainage pathways stay open is so important. Luckily, there are many drainage outlets in the human body. The lymphatic system is one of them. Our body can also remove toxins through our skin, urinary tract, digestive, respiratory, and circulatory systems.

The lymphatic system and a few other organs are really the workhorses that help keep our toxicity levels low. We can give these organs a hand by doing a few things at home to lighten the load on our bodies.

Start by eliminating toxic, daily-use skincare products, which have been linked to hormone disruption and fertility issues. These products include deodorants, shampoos, body washes, and even makeup.

Ditch the plastic Tupperware® containers and your Teflon pans! Scented plug-ins and room sprays should be a thing of the past. Using a dry brush and implementing a daily lymphatic massage routine can be quite beneficial to your body, and drinking plenty of water will flush out any unwanted toxins and chemicals you may be exposing yourself to.

The good news is, once identified, your body can correct these stressor(s) through safe, natural, nutritional means, allowing a return to optimal health and the ability to maintain it.

While there is never a good time to start, and many make excuses throughout the week and push off important health matters, it's essential to embark on the journey to be your healthiest self. Most of my clients come to me as a last resort. I would love to help as many people as possible before they reach that point. Simple lifestyle changes can go such a long way.

Finally, Relief!

One of our clients at Natural Connections was suffering from severe stomach issues for over a year. They had seen all the specialists you could think of prior to coming into our office. Lactose intolerance, frequent trips to the bathroom, and the occasional eczema flare-ups made their life difficult to manage. After just six weeks of being seen in our office, they finally started to feel like themselves again.

Many people who come to us have suffered from migraines, dizziness, infertility, weight issues, chronic fatigue, and more. These clients have done very well on their programs and have seen tremendous results in just a brief period. They are dedicated to feeling better and really put the time and effort in to do so, and it happens!

Treatment options differ for everyone. Sometimes, a stressor can be negated through a simple 90-day food elimination and whole-food supplements to better support the body.

> **Again, we do not guess; we test. It's the best way to narrow down a specific program for your needs. Skip the fad diets that never work long-term. Our protocol is tailored exactly for you.**

Picture an onion with many layers. As you go through our program, each layer unfolds. When we dial into what's going on with your body to help bring it back to its optimal function, we call it the "Fine-Tuning" phase.

Are you ready to take that heavy load off your shoulders and finally put your needs and health first? Are you ready to fine-tune yourself? Find Natural Connections on Instagram at natural_connections_lbi or send an email to natural connectionslbi@gmail.com

About the Author

Brianna Frost-Smith is a certified Nutrition Response Testing®
practitioner with Natural Connections in Ship Bottom, New
Jersey. Her deep passion for healthcare led to her certification
through the ULAN program. She strives to reach people on their
wellness journeys before they become sick.

Brianna grew up loving nature and anything to do with the
outdoors. She loves hunting and fishing and plans on teaching
her children the same. She has a small homestead, homeschools
her kiddos, and is married to her best friend. Brianna believes
that everything happens for a reason and that God has led her
down this path, so she can help many others. When not working
to help people feel their best, she loves to travel and seek out new
places with new faces. Traveling the world with her children to
show them what life is all about is a dream she will make come
true.

CHAPTER 8

Her Money, Her Power: Why We Need More Money in Women's Hands

Yahaira Krahmer

"A woman's best protection is a little money of her own."
—Clare Boothe Luce

Some will tell you that money is the root of all evil. That it's dirty, only understood by men, or not for us women to be concerned with.

As women, we grow up as children watching our mothers and following in our grandmother's footsteps. The cycle goes like this: Grow up, graduate college, get a survival job, find a good husband, and raise children.

Rinse and repeat.

Well, I'm here to tell you that is not how your life needs to play out. As women, our biggest asset is our knowledge of the world around us, and that includes our financial sense. You see, money is energy. But more than that, money is power, community, security, a door-opener, and a barrier-buster.

Having the right mindset and money goals allow you to create a world you never imagined was remotely possible. The trouble is that not enough women realize the tremendous impact of taking control of their financial lives. Today, too many women come from toxic relationships, broken homes, or lack the proper education to stay out of debt. They succumb to poor habits that leave their credit profiles demolished and resign themselves to a life of mediocrity.

My Roots

As a young girl growing up in a "tough" part of the Bronx, New York, I watched my parents run a grocery store business around the clock, where the amount of time spent in the business didn't quite correlate with the amount brought in. The constant narrative was "Money is hard to come by," "You have to work very hard for your money," or simply "We don't have enough."

The story I grew up with around money profoundly shaped the way I approached life, work, and my value. I internalized the belief that I had to constantly outwork myself, always pushing harder, always proving my worth. If I wasn't grinding, I feared I'd be seen as lazy or undeserving of what I earned. Working hard for money was so ingrained that I struggled to even comprehend making money in a way that wasn't directly tied to effort, sweat, and sacrifice.

Like many in their generation, my parents' mindset made passive income seem alien, almost dishonest.

I couldn't wrap my head around the idea that money could work for me instead of the other way around.

For years, I rejected opportunities that didn't align with that old-school, hustle-obsessed narrative. Then, slowly but surely, I began to understand that true financial freedom doesn't come from endlessly chasing the next paycheck. It comes from learning how to make your money work harder than you do.

I now realize that wealth isn't just about the grind; it's about being smart, strategic, and intentional with your resources. It's not about working yourself to the bone but learning to leverage time, energy, and, yes, money to create lasting value. Years later, I've finally unlearned my limiting beliefs, and now I'm focused on building wealth to align with freedom, not exhaustion. True freedom comes from taking control, not only of your life but of your financial future.

After my epiphany, I had to help the next generation of women take back control of their destinies by teaching them self-empowerment through financial education, business ownership, and changing that narrative. These were powerful tools they could wield to build the life they deserved.

Watching my mother navigate the exhausting demands of running her business while struggling to find the financial guidance and support she so desperately needed was a turning point for me. She worked tirelessly, pouring her heart and soul into her business, but lacked the financial knowledge to fully thrive.

Her challenges became another one of my motivations. Through those experiences, I discovered a gift for numbers and strategy that I would pass on to others to make a difference.

Building Your Best Financial Self

I launched my accounting and consulting firm with one clear goal in mind: to empower women like my mother, women who work hard but need the right guidance to build sustainable, profitable businesses. I wanted to be the support system they never had—the one to help them make sense of the financial side of things and give them the confidence to grow, succeed, and finally take charge of their financial futures. Because when women are empowered with financial knowledge, they aren't just building businesses—they are building legacies.

> **I'm a firm believer that women are meant to be trailblazers, visionaries, and masters of their own lives.**

Jessica

During the early years of my business, I got the opportunity to work with a talented creative named Jessica. When Jessica and I met via a Zoom meeting, she was filled with self-doubt, which she had internalized over the years. She often repeated phrases like "I'm not good with numbers." Her husband had managed their finances, and she managed the household and kids. Jessica felt guilty for thinking something was missing in her life even though she had it all by society's standards—the husband, kids, and white picket fence.

Jessica had a brilliant business idea and the passion to make it a success, but she lacked the financial literacy and guidance to launch it.

Our journey began with my sharing basic financial education, from refining her offers and pricing for profit to creating a business spending plan. Over the course of two years, her sales increased to six figures and profits of more than 50%. Jessica started taking charge of her finances.

The confidence that came with this knowledge empowered Jessica to make decisions that had once felt out of reach, including making business investments and participating actively in her family's finances. Jessica didn't succumb to society's idea that a woman cannot have it all; she proved that a woman can be an outstanding mother, wife, businesswoman, philanthropist, and anything else she aspires to be.

Stressed-Out Sofia

Another former client of mine, Sofia, came to me overwhelmed and confused about how to move forward financially during a contentious divorce.

Sofia had been kept in the dark for so long as her partner never involved her in the finances, so she was unaware of their financial standing. While working together, she learned to understand key metrics in financial statements and what documents were important in determining a fair divorce settlement.

We started from scratch—budgets, financial reports, you name it. It wasn't just about learning the ropes but about rewriting her identity from passive observer to proactive powerhouse.

Fast forward five years and Sofia now runs a successful consulting business that employs five, and she serves as a board member of a local non-profit organization for battered women. In Sofia's case (which is the case for many), financial literacy is not just about dollars and cents, but it is the key to unlocking a new path away from toxic or undermining relationships/environments.

The change was transformative for both of these clients, which is a testament to how financial literacy can create a profound personal and professional liberation.

I could tell countless stories of women just like Jessica and Sofia. In many instances, I've been honored to help turn a burning idea into a full-fledged business, creating generational wealth that benefits local communities and gives women the power they deserve.

As I work with women every day through my accounting and consulting firm, I am consistently reminded of how transformative financial literacy and smart business strategies can be. Every woman's journey is different, but the core principles of success remain the same. Whether they're just starting their business or scaling to new heights, I always share with them five essential tips that I believe are non-negotiable for building a thriving and sustainable business:

1. **Set Measurable Financial Goals** - Identify short- and long-term financial goals such as saving $10,000, paying off $6,000 in credit card debt, investing $500/month, etc.

2. **Build an Emergency Cushion** - Aim to stash at least 6-12 months of expenses in a separate bank account that only you can access, which will serve as a financial safety net in case of unexpected circumstances/financial hardship.

3. **Invest and Plan for Your Future** - Invest as early as possible, regardless of the amount—your future self will thank you later.

4. **Create a Spending Plan** - Review your expenses for the last 12 months (both personal and business) to better understand your spending habits. Create a spending plan that aligns with your goals. Review monthly and adjust as needed.

5. **Seek Professional Support** - Surround yourself with people who have your best interests at heart and can be a sounding board for your financial goals and plans.

Today, women are not merely participating; they are leading and paving roads for others. Yet, despite the progress that has been made, a significant challenge remains: gender equality.

According to the National Association of Women Business Owners, over 14 million women-owned businesses in the United States generate more than $2.7 trillion in annual revenue. [9] While these figures are undeniably impressive, they are lacking significantly compared to businesses operated by men. Despite the progress women have made, men still own or hold leadership positions in **6 out of every 10 companies** and continue to receive a disproportionately higher share of funding—those numbers have got to change!

> **When we educate a woman in the art of finance, you don't just change her world—you change *the* world.**

Imagine if the numbers I shared above increased exponentially for women business owners. Can you picture the impact?

More money in the hands of women isn't just money spent but rather invested. It boosts communities and seeds businesses that fill the gaps in society. Having supported over 100 women-owned businesses, I've seen firsthand how outstanding women go beyond economic contributions to transform their local communities and set the foundation for wider change.

I hope this chapter, along with the stories of the incredible women shared in this book, inspire you to make one simple yet profoundly important decision today: **take control of your money.** No matter where you stand financially at this moment—whether you feel like you're thriving or just trying to make ends

---

9 "2024 Impact of Women-Owned Businesses Research." WEI. Accessed September 13, 2024. https://www.wippeducationinstitute.org/2024-impact-of-women-owned-businesses.

meet—the great news is this: **you hold the power** to completely transform the trajectory of your financial future.

Every financial decision you make, every habit you cultivate starting today has the potential to shift your life in extraordinary ways. The steps you take right now are not just about paying off debt or saving a little more—they are about establishing a future of financial independence, security, and possibility. You have the power to turn your financial story into one of empowerment, freedom, and success.

The path to financial freedom isn't a distant dream reserved for a select few—it's a series of daily choices, each moving you closer to the life you truly deserve. **And that power? It's already within you.**

So, ask yourself: **What story do you want your finances to tell five years from now?** Will it be one of struggle or strength? The decision is yours.

To learn more about Yahaira and how she can help you transform your business, visit: www.accounther.com.

About the Author

Yahaira Krahmer is a business finance expert and the visionary founder of AccountHer, an innovative accounting and financial coaching firm dedicated to empowering women entrepreneurs. With over a decade of experience, Yahaira has made it her life's mission to help women take charge of their financial futures, break through traditional barriers, and build thriving, profitable businesses that stand the test of time.

Her approach goes beyond the numbers—she offers personalized financial strategies designed to meet each client's unique needs, paired with insightful guidance and unwavering support. Whether developing tailored financial roadmaps or coaching women through the complexities of entrepreneurship, Yahaira is passionate about seeing her clients succeed in business and life. Her work has enabled countless women to master their finances, reclaim power, and achieve financial independence with fierce confidence.

Residing in New Jersey with her husband, two children, and beloved dog, Zoe, Yahaira remains committed to her mission of women empowerment and gender equality. When she's not helping women unlock their financial potential, you can find her enjoying the outdoors with her family or traveling the world.

CHAPTER 9

Leaping Into a Heart–Centered Business

Ilissa Goman

"Everyone has oceans to fly if they have the heart to do it. Is it reckless? Maybe. But what do dreams know of boundaries?"
—Amelia Earhart

R ecently, after my niece's birth, I was looking through a hoard of family photos from my childhood, searching for a specific photo to give my sister. In my digging around, I came across a photo of myself that I absolutely adore. I was probably just shy of two, and the sparkle in my eyes, the pure love, and innocence in that moment were full of laughter and fun.

That's quite a contrast to a handful of years ago when I saw this photo, and it made me sad. *Where did that girl go?* She has gone through so much since then. The hurt made her quiet and not trust people. It made her not trust herself.

I had built walls so high that I didn't even know they existed. They were so tall; I had no idea I had imprisoned myself.

I spent every day trying to keep the peace or get by. Keeping up with the busy work of life: Business, husband, child, and home. I was treading water.

One day, I wanted to drown.

That was the day I turned everything around, the day I started on my big healing journey. I knew things had to change; they couldn't stay the same, or I wouldn't be here for my daughter.

I started my new journey using the typical surface-level healing methods: working on my mindset, trusting the Universe, using vision boards, and exercising.

Even though they were shallow, I needed these baby steps to get me going in the right direction. I needed to see things getting better.

And they did.

New opportunities came my way. My businesses started to really work. I had fresh energy, having moved back into that positive, forward-thinking mindset.

But I knew my real demons—all the trauma I hadn't dealt with—were still there. I had lived through every kind of abuse you can think of, tied in with bullying, being in a marriage I no longer wanted, suffering a miscarriage, and more.

I tried so often to put those events and people out of my mind. I had forgiven all who had wronged me. I told myself *so many other people have it worse, so who am I to complain? Aren't I supposed to be grateful for what I have?* I know you've probably had these same thoughts.

Around this time, I came across a post from an amazing person in a Facebook business growth group, Natasha Bray. She had a similar backstory to mine, which gave me so much hope. If she had risen above her trauma, so could I. I just knew it in my bones.

I took a huge leap then and decided to invest in myself and her healing program, the *Ultimate Uplevel Academy (UUA)*. The program was all about healing your inner self to achieve success in your work. It was the first time I had ever invested in myself without placing another Band-Aid on my business.

Through Natasha's teachings, I uncovered that I had unintentionally created huge blocks around me to prevent receiving success, love, and more. These walls around my heart kept me safe. And they kept me small.

I ended up going through the UUA a few times to keep peeling back the layers, going deeper in my healing (more on that later).

One of the rounds I signed up for came with an offer for a package of one-on-one sessions with one of Natasha's lead HeartHealing® therapists, Kirsty Wick.

I trusted my gut again and registered, although I was a little nervous because I am not a fan of traditional therapy. I had done quite a bit of that as a teen, and it was never my gig.

Before my sessions, I had started doing a ton of healing work within the UUA, which had brought me to new levels. But I still didn't want to touch the really hard stuff. Kirsty smoothed the way to delve into it and heal.

The initial intake form made it easy to open up freely and describe exactly what I wanted to change and my vision for myself, as it allowed me to more comfortably reveal my past traumas. The audio I was assigned before the session eased me into working with Kirsty. These sessions were just over an hour apiece, and after each, I felt much lighter and more at peace. Listening to my recorded Heart Imprints afterward helped solidify our healing work and (bonus!) I could return to them as needed.

The HeartHealing® sessions were exactly what my soul craved. I was given a safe place to break down all my walls and reconnect to my real self. It was like taking a sledgehammer out and being done with the old me.

The one truth people don't talk about when it comes to healing is that once you've done significant work, you will realize you've stripped off all those "protective" layers and are now standing there naked. All the shoulds and supposed tos are gone, but what is left?

An all-new you. A fresh start.

After my intense, real healing began, I kept myself in a pretty calm state for a little while. I had broken free of my marriage, was on my own for the very first time in my life, and had started dating again (highly *don't* recommend, LOL). I was also spending time deeply connecting with my daughter. My work life was steady and growing at a nice pace, but I knew something big was coming.

I've always had a gut feeling I was meant for more. Instinctively, I knew I had to keep going, persevere, and pivot when necessary. I had to trust my bigger vision.

In 2022, the title of my book came to me. For some time, I knew I wanted to write it. It would be about my struggles with emotional addictions—that surface-level living I was so good at. I wanted to show other people they could get through their trauma and pain, too.

I spent a few weeks in the springtime writing the first part of the book. It was definitely a therapeutic experience. I gave myself grace and space and did not rush it.

Before long, *Now Leaving Numb* was born. Later that year, a local artist worked with me on the visual guide to accompany the reader's journey through the book. My vision was blossoming.

By the end of the summer of 2023, my book was out into the world, hitting the best-seller category on launch day within hours. The reviews and feedback were incredible.

But something happened when I was writing it. I noticed I was talking a lot about the surface-level healing I was doing with my clients then. Yes, I was still playing it safe and small.

Now, even though the work I was doing was incredible, I felt a disconnect between my true self, a missing piece. I had worked for years as a brand strategist, with a side of creative design while leading a team of women. Hell, I could create an entire business in a day after a deep dive with a client, including the concept, logo, website home page mock, and product suite ideas. It seemed this would be my success path.

What else was out there for me?

While writing my book, Natasha again opened enrollment for her HeartHealing® practitioners certification program. There was that gut feeling I couldn't shake. I had looked at the program a number of times yet always stopped myself because I wasn't a "healer." That sounded way too woo-woo for me. Now, it suddenly sounded different. If I was going to do this, I had to fully dedicate myself to it as it would be a long process, with many hours of training and more healing work on myself.

On top of this, it would be a total career shift. *What will everyone think? How will this impact the business and work relationships I have spent so much time building?*

I decided to take the leap.

I am so, so glad I did.

While training and navigating this new "naked" space, I dug further into my Human Design. It was fascinating. My Human Design shone a light on how different activities can either brighten me or drain my energy. Human Design is a system that was created to help you identify the various ways energy best moves through your body. It will give you insights into your decision-making, career paths, your best environments, and more. It is a mix of a handful of different ideologies and is so spot on for myself and the friends' and clients' charts I have studied.

I also started studying my astrological charts after a mentor told me, "You have a lot of 8th-house planet placements." If you don't know, the 8th house is associated with transformation, intimacy, legacy, and magic. Hearing this was incredibly validating and reaffirmed my decision to become a HeartHealing® practitioner.

For a long time, I had no idea of the magic I possessed. Yet, I knew it was there. I see people on a soul level. I know the possibilities within you and how to make you see and believe in them, too. This is a huge gift for the people I work with. I had no idea that not everyone could access this insight.

In finding myself in this naked but building phase, I also explored what my trauma was covering—my blossoming abilities that were now coming out since I was taking the time to heal.

I wondered *how can I really tap into that intuition now that I am trusting myself and giving myself the time I need?* Understanding how my energy works as an empath and Projector (a Human Design identity) is a major key to my happiness, success, and how I best function within spaces and my work. As a Projector, I had to learn how not to force things, to give them space and let them come to me, to know my power and authentic self is my innate magnetism to the right people. Projectors work best in their wisdom and not on a huge production scale.

When your brain is trying to run from trauma, it doesn't have the space to show you your gifts or the abilities to develop them.

You might have glimpses of your talents that keep you moving forward, but you have to do the healing work to give them the space to expand and explode in the best ways.

A big lesson I must leave you with is that healing is not a small or linear process; in fact, I believe it never ends. The intensity slows as you heal, but you will always encounter new situations. Healing allows you to navigate these situations with grace and the faith in yourself that you will get through it and not numb out. Healing is layered.

You will encounter situations where the old you would've done something so differently than the you who stands here today, and future you would do it even more differently. Stand in your power and trust that if you are doing your best, then you are taking the right action at the right time.

How do you know it's time to start doing healing work for yourself? Maybe you're finally sick of your own shit. You know you need to make a change and are ready for it. Just simply decide to start, then stand in your power to move forward.

When you are ready to embrace transformation, you will see incredible results.

These five fears most commonly hold back my clients: 1) failure, 2) rejection, 3) vulnerability, 4) the unknown, and 5) losing control. Was that a gut punch? Do you see yourself in one or more of these five fears?

If you keep asking yourself, *when will it be my turn?* Here's your answer: Now. Now is your time.

Are you ready?

You might have hope for a different life for yourself, but are you ready to have faith? Faith requires your belief in yourself to be so strong that you take actual action. Faith means you will face those fears, and you may be terrified, but you have the unshakable belief you will come out the other side.

Someone asked me recently, "What do you do for work?" I answered, "I just started working with people with this really cool new healing technique ...." But the very first thought that came to mind was, *whatever the fuck I want.* And it is true.

I follow my heart.

I live without regrets.

I live full of passion.

I live full of love.

It is absolutely amazing to hear from clients that they have turned down a romantic relationship after noticing red flags or that they didn't feel tethered to stay in an abusive situation out of codependency. It is incredibly empowering to see a client's business unfold in the most magical of ways, making them shine even brighter and bringing success in unexpected experiences. I love hearing about clients on massive career-goal trajectories, blazing new paths forward they never thought possible.

The new me has made peace with the old me. She will always be a part of my world, but I have adapted and healed enough to live with her and give her grace and love for what she didn't know and what she endured. But the pain she weathered has no place here. I will no longer allow it to lash me down and prevent me from flying.

Knowing and living what is on the other side in my new skin is irresistible. It keeps me right where I am supposed to be: showing women that their destinies are revealed when they heal. Seeing they are even more joyful and promising than the trauma that colored them gray is indescribable. Now, I embrace color so much, the representation of my gratitude and full heart, that I had a rainbow tutu made. I don't mind telling you that every single woman who lays eyes on it wants to try it on. I'm even wearing it on the cover of my book. Magic is contagious.

Please join me at www.ilissag.com for more information on HeartHealing® sessions and other fun ways to work with me. Always reach out if you have any questions; I'm a frequent flier on Instagram.

About the Author

Ilissa Goman is a multi-level certified HeartHealing™ practitioner dedicated to helping women entrepreneurs heal at a soul level and break through the emotional and mental blocks preventing them from receiving everything they desire. With her expertise in HeartHealing™ and intuitive gifts, Ilissa offers a unique approach to guiding clients toward authentic success and fulfillment in business and life.

Ilissa's deep passion for helping women reclaim their authentic selves stems from her own transformative journey of overcoming emotional addiction and trauma. This journey inspired her to develop the SELFF method, a practical and empowering framework that has helped countless women reignite their passion for their work and unlock their full potential.

In addition to her healing work, Ilissa is the best-selling author of *Now Leaving Numb*, detailing her personal story and insights into emotional healing and entrepreneurship.

Ilissa lives in upstate New York with her beloved daughter, enjoying the serenity of nature and embracing the joys of family life. She is committed to helping others heal their hearts, transform their lives, and create a legacy they can be proud of.

CHAPTER 10

The Reinvention of the Mompreneur: Personal Branding with Empowerment

Clara Wang

"Don't be afraid to reinvent your life. You're not starting over; you're starting with experience."
—Mel Robbins

"So, what do you do, now?" asked an ex-coworker as he towered over me—male, single, dressed to impress in a designer suit. I was at some frivolous ex-coworker reunion party held at a fancy restaurant in the city. It felt like he was asking a trick question.

I remember squirming in my itchy maternity dress. My little ones were at home with a babysitter that evening while I was there at this party, fulfilling zero purpose besides missing their bedtime snuggles. I silently scolded myself for coming. I didn't even work there anymore.

A tightness closed my throat as I barely got the words out. "Oh, I'm just a mom now. Director of operations at 'the circus,' ha, ha, ha," as I stupidly gestured air quotes.

Just a mom?!

I felt regret the minute I heard those words coming out of my mouth. I had betrayed myself . . . and a majority of the female population.

My face was burning. I couldn't tell if it was guilt, shame, or both.

How did being "just a mom" become so diminished and un-substantial? "Just-a-moms" are women whose bodies have endured the pains of child-bearing, who are diehards providing a safe and healthy living for their families, who fight to maintain the mental load of parenting, and who lay down the groundwork for strong, healthy, and happy individuals and communities—all the while facing society's pressure of constant comparisons to other women for what they have, what they do, or who they are.

I should be standing in complete solidarity with all the "just-a-moms"!

"Oh, okay. That's great." No follow-up question came from my former co-worker as we both awkwardly shifted away to find something else to occupy ourselves. He was no longer interested. I remember standing there feeling judged for "giving up," becoming lost and unseen.

As I looked around the room, it felt as though I was peering in from the outside. All these "employees" climbing up the corporate ladder. I so passionately used to be one of them. My academic achievements and corporate titles were my accolades. Being one of the few women leaders in a sea of male counterparts was my badge of honor.

At one point, I was even deemed too demanding because I completed all the tasks my male counterparts did and more—in heels. During one of my performance reviews, my boss—male, married with no children, told me I was doing great and deserved the salary bump he presented. But he also blatantly pointed out that I should expect challenging times ahead simply because I was a petite-sized minority with a "high and squeaky" voice that did not command leadership. Pointless feminist criticism like this leaves a lasting mark on one.

And so it begins, that slow mental accumulation of self-doubt and imposter syndrome. Oh, but I buckled down and pushed on harder, advancing that ladder, shaking off that negative voice. I was a young and single corporate shining star with no other worries in the world.

Fast forward a couple of years later; I was in a boardroom meeting. A statistic chart proclaimed a glaring downward red arrow. The head of human resources had just declared that the biggest employment drainer was "maternity leave." He said bitterly, "These women, they get married, have their children, and then they leave the work force. They leave to the *other side*." As though women making decisions to focus on raising children were such an inconvenience to the company and society.

Now, here I am on the *"other side"* because I started a family.

But wait, how did I end up in this position after all that hard work? Why does it have to be this side or the *other* side? Then I remembered I *had* to choose.

This is not a conversation about the working mom versus the stay-at-home mom but rather about the way our society has simply been unkind, especially to women who are caregivers and want to work and pursue personal goals. This is a conversation about how motherhood and caregiving are possibly the toughest responsibilities in life. Yet, somehow, the math never adds up. The lack of support and sad reality of the structure work against the ability of women to do both: caregiving and having a career. Society is determined to make women choose.

As so many other women have and will, I chose to place my career and personal goals on hold to focus on motherhood for some years. It was what worked for our family and financial abilities. Everyone's situation is different. I recognize I am fortunate to have a partner in life who supported our family and allowed me to have this choice. Not all women do.

A 2023 State of Motherhood survey polled by Motherly, an advocacy group, showed that nearly 25% of American mothers identified as a stay-at-home parent, a sharp rise from 15% in 2022.[10] They called it the great resignation for mothers; the top reasons women chose this route were the lack of flexible work schedules and affordable childcare.

Corporate workplace structures are simply not sustainable for a family with childcare needs—salaries do not support the high

---

10   "State of Motherhood." Motherly, May 8, 2024. https://www.mother.ly/state-of-motherhood/.

cost of outside childcare; inflexible working hours go against the ability to manage childcare and household management. In fact, in that same Motherly survey, 82% of moms under 30 say childcare is their primary reason for considering leaving the workforce; 50% of non-working moms point to affordable childcare as the prerequisite for returning to or entering the workforce.

If stay-at-home were a professionally recognized and paid job, the median annual salary would be over $184,820, working an average of 106 hours per week, 15 hours a day, 7 days a week, with no vacation days and no health benefits.[11] Working moms are said to spend an average of 54 hours per week managing childcare and household management, in addition to their regular working hours and expensive outside childcare costs when they are away from their children.[12] A US Department of Labor analysis shows the cost of childcare has risen 115% since 2000, estimating a single child can cost up to 19% of the median family income.[13] Additionally, 66% of mothers are paying more than $1,000 per month for childcare.[14]

That math really doesn't add up.

---

11 "How Much Should a Stay-at-Home Mom Make." Salary.com, May 5, 2021. https://www.salary.com/articles/how-much-is-a-mom-really-worth-the-amount-may-surprise-you/.
12 "How Much Should a Stay-at-Home Mom Make." Salary.com, May 5, 2021. https://www.salary.com/articles/how-much-is-a-mom-really-worth-the-amount-may-surprise-you/.
13 Zinkula, Jacob. "Childcare Is about to Get Even More Expensive at the End of September Unless Congress Acts." Business Insider. Accessed October 1, 2024. https://www.businessinsider.com/childcare-costs-expensive-rising-2023-6#:~.
14 "State of Motherhood." Motherly, May 8, 2024. https://www.mother.ly/state-of-motherhood/.

It takes nine months to grow a human inside a woman's body. Whether she labors for a few hours or a few days to deliver the baby, her body goes through a trauma. A full recovery takes at least six months, not taking into consideration postpartum complications and caring for a newborn baby. And yet, women are only given three months off from work to recover if they're lucky as they settle into a new lifestyle . . . all while likely not having a source of income.

While things have started to progress a little over the years, with more corporate companies participating in progressive health benefits for women, the United States remains the only high-income country not to offer federal paid maternity leave. Paid maternity leave is guaranteed in 178 countries; the United States is not one of them.

Many women are faced with these life-changing choices that most men are exempted from. And because of these choices, women are no longer entitled to equal benefits.

Remember that glaring red downward arrow in the boardroom?

If women choose to be stay-at-home parents, they will give up their careers. If they choose to continue working, they are not a good mom. It's not our fault, yet we are constantly expected to do it all (if you want to). And if you can't, you're either not up for it or not trying hard enough.

Is this it? Is it selfish to want more? Is it okay to believe I can have both and more? Is this being un-motherly?

The New York Times once coined the term "languishing" as the COVID-lockdown-induced dominant emotion of 2021, calling it something along the lines of the in-between of flourishing and depression. "It wasn't burnout—we still had energy. It wasn't depression—we didn't feel hopeless. We just felt somewhat joyless and aimless, a sense of stagnation and emptiness."[15]

The description of this feeling was all too eerily familiar, triggering memories of heaviness, blankness, and the lingering guilt of even daring to feel a tad "languished."

This "languish" is not new—the sense of mundane and a need for *more*. There is a predominant group of people who have lived through/are living it/and will live through it, with or without a pandemic— yup, those "just-a-moms."

Women who have set careers and goals aside to focus on motherhood experience the "bloom" in mom life and yet find it startlingly sprinkled with moments of "*Is this really it?*" When moms start feeling the need to move forward for something more—an even better life for themselves and their families—a mompreneur is made. Mompreneurs want to stay the nurturer for their children, and at the same time, they want to reach personal goals to make a difference in their lives and others. They want to solve a need and close a gap, to strive for financial freedom, and to do it all on their terms. This is where strength, self-awareness, and confidence grow. It is the recognition of this

---

15 Grant, Adam. "There's a Name for the Blah You're Feeling: It's Called Languishing." The New York Times, April 19, 2021. https://www.nytimes.com/2021/04/19/well/mind/covid-mental-health-languishing.html.

languishing and the need to harness it that leads to becoming a Mompreneur.

Now that we can put a name to this uneasy feeling, it makes dealing with it easier. Also, at least now the world can understand why mompreneurs are made—making the math add up as much as possible.

> **Mom·pre·neur /mämprə́nər/: "A woman who sets up and runs her own business in addition to caring for her young child or children." (Google/Oxford Languages definition.)**

I identify as a mompreneur because the importance of thriving in both mom life and in my career is my personal goal. I want to be a mom and run a successful business that helps others but on my terms. It's a reinvention of myself using my past experiences to create the flexibility I need and the freedom to create with my skills.

As women, we are told to fit into certain limiting and outdated boxes. We are all uniquely ever-evolving into who we are and who we can be. Having that kind of control is empowering, and it's possible for any woman.

> **Personal fulfillment is allowed and a necessity to be a better mom, wife, daughter, and community member. It is not easy, but it certainly doesn't have to be one or the other.**

Unlike working in corporate America, as a mompreneur, I have discovered your identity should not be solely dependent on what you do or your "title." It should include who you are and your why. We should not have to choose to be one or the other. It is time for women to stand together and break these binary thoughts.

According to the Japanese, everyone has an ikigai–a reason for living. And the residents of the Japanese island of Okinawa—home to the world's longest-living people—note that finding it is the key to a happier and longer life. Osaka University academic researcher Noriyuki Nakanishi is a prolific author appearing in multiple publications and explains, "*Ikigai gives individuals a sense of a life worth living. It is not necessarily related to economic status. Ikigai is personal; it reflects the inner self of an individual and expresses that faithfully. It establishes a unique mental world in which the individual can feel at ease.*"

Simply put, ikigai means figuring out these four guiding questions:

1. What do you love?
2. What are you good at?
3. What does the world need?
4. What can you be paid for?

I discovered that my ikigai is to use my love for photography, storytelling, and creativity and combine it with my experiences and skills. It is for me to support other women also seeking fulfillment as mompreneurs as they evolve and progress toward their goals. We need to help more women build that bridge linking mom life and business and achieve a happier, healthier, fulfilled life—getting them out of the "just-a-mom" mindset.

So, despite that squirmy moment at the reunion party many moons ago—little did I know that a few years later, when I was finally ready to stop languishing—I was right—there is more for me.

Becoming a mompreneur doesn't happen overnight, and there will be many hard days. The self-doubt and imposter syndrome that may have piled up over the years will continue to exist. The balance will always be challenging but not impossible. When I finally picked up my courage, a camera, and my fanaticism for attention to detail (thanks to the nature of my corporate job) allowed me to launch a business buoyed by a love of photography and storytelling.

As I invested in self-development and learning new skills in photography, marketing, and storytelling, I made it my mission to help mompreneurs build a thriving life for themselves through brand photography. Because I get it, too, and when you know you're not alone in this feeling, you feel seen. It is also why so many mompreneurs love supporting other mompreneurs. It's better than staying in a state of languish alone.

While I am not a life or business coach, I am a good storyteller. As a personal brand photographer, I wholeheartedly believe in photos going beyond empowering a woman's business and herself. They not only strategically market the type of business and center on her journey toward fulfillment—a beautiful medley of who she is, what she has created, how she wants to show up, and why she is doing it—a mompreneur is precisely the amalgamation of all the different "titles" that make her uniquely who she is. One title doesn't have to be before the other, either. That's part of the beauty of the mompreneur.

Whether a woman is starting a business or returning to work outside the home, the combination of her skills, experiences, and personality, who she is, how others perceive her, and how she wants to be perceived is what matters.

No matter the type of photography, I always begin the conversation by exploring a woman's sense of identity through the expression of her personal brand. I capture in photos the story she tells about herself, both to the world and herself.

Focus on this, and you will feel seen. You will grow into a sense of belonging—essential for human survival and fulfilling basic psychological needs and emotional health—as it supports your social ability to thrive individually and within communities.

Every day, I am still stumbling and finding my way along this journey, but I've met so many like-minded women who have not only given me comradeship but immense support and motivation I am forever grateful for.

Join me on this journey to stand up against society coercing us into putting limits on ourselves as women. Be a mom now; be an entrepreneur later. Do it at the same time. It's your choice. Life is but a series of ebbs and flows.

Use brand photography as reminders and communication platforms to make your business mission and personal goals crystal clear and strengthen your impact. Lift more women out of the languish cloud; push more mompreneurs toward success, and ask better questions when you meet a woman for the first time. "What do you *like* to do?" versus "What do you do?"

Finally, stick with the people who pull the magic out of you, not the madness. Spreading energy and breaking stereotypes for all women is pure empowerment.

> *"Reinvention of the mompreneur—stop trying to fit*
> *yourself into boxes created by others. You don't have to*
> *start over. Make your own circles with what you love, and*
> *bedazzle it with your light."*
> —Clara Wang

With a Brand Image Library, you will always feel confident marketing your business and personal brand. You can find Clara at: www.clarawangphotography.com

About the Author

Clara Wang is a New Jersey-based brand photographer, storyteller, content creator, and creative entrepreneur. She is also a mom of two young boys—meaning she is also a circus director, personal chauffeur, private chef . . .

In her previous work as a specialist in the hospitality industry, managing consistent excellence and product quality was her jam. She cultivated the strong belief that the little things can make the biggest difference . . . resulting in the most flawless customer experience. Today, she weaves her love of photography and storytelling together to deliver the highest-quality images for you to use in all your brand product marketing efforts.

As Your Brand Photographer and go-to visual content partner whose specialty is a year-long retainer service delivering strategic photo content that captures the product story and founder story, Clara shines the light on your craft and trade. Her whole package approach allows brands to stand out and scale faster across various marketing channels. She believes that photography should grow and progress with your business and needs constant refreshment, so you never feel the frustration of not having that "right" photo to use.

Born in Singapore, Clara grew up globe-trotting with her adventurous parents and eventually landed in New Jersey, which she now calls home. When not shooting photos, you'll probably find her savoring new and delicious foods in restaurants or her husband's cooking, watching rom-coms on Netflix, glass of wine in hand, or whisking her three boys (including her husband) away on their next global excursion.

CHAPTER 11

Secrets to Building an Amazing Career on Your Terms

Nora Gillis

*"Well, you've got dreams, and you know they matter. Be
your own boss, climb your own ladder."*
—Dolly Parton, 9 to 5

As I write this, I am preparing to go skydiving on Sunday. By the way, you should know that I am absolutely terrified of heights.

I'm talking about the kind of fear that has me backing into the only solid wall in a glass elevator, where I might close my eyes for the duration of the ride up or down (up seems scarier for some reason).

So why am I doing this? Great question.

Despite my fear, I also feel the thrill of pushing myself past it to experience what is both exciting and terrifying.

Will it be as scary as changing my career path and coming out from hiding behind my computer and Excel spreadsheets to speak in front of several hundred people, most of whom are men frequently convinced they know the topic better than me?

I will have to report back on that in the next book ....

The Hamster Maze

I wanted to write about successfully navigating the world of corporate careers because I love my job. Not every day, or every aspect of it, and not all the time, but enough to share what has worked for me, so maybe it can work for you.

Throughout my journey, I have created connections with so many amazing people and learned lots of fascinating facts, like there is a lot of creativity involved in the financial services industry despite its boring and dry image.

My career trajectory has been surprising and unexpected, mostly to me.

Like so many do, I crafted an image of myself I held onto tightly and organized everything else around. The trouble with that approach is that all facets of us evolve and change. Plus, we don't actually know ourselves as well as we think. Like a sunflower, we keep stretching up and moving our focus toward the sun always shifting through the sky; it's different every day. One day, we are tiny seedlings, and then we find ourselves tall and proud, gravitating toward our authentic interests. If we turned away from that bright light that calls us and stayed in the same place, we would shrink and struggle.

What I do in my current financial services industry role varies depending on the day and who you ask. One way to explain it is that I talk to people for a living. Another is that I am a connector: I connect the right ideas and solutions to any client situation a financial advisor might be dealing with, or I connect people to each other.

Some might simply say that I'm in sales, but that approach misrepresents how I do my job.

I like people, pretty much all of them. And I like seeing them succeed and reach their goals and dreams, because that gives me the satisfaction of a job well done. Whether it's my financial advisor clients growing their business and successfully helping people enjoy retirement or my team learning skills and stepping into new roles, seeing that success is why I love my job.

Back to the concept of evolving . . . .

The bottom line is that I had absolutely no idea my job existed while I was in college and early in my career. Even when I first encountered the men in this role (and it *is* incredibly male-dominated), it seemed the exact opposite of what I might enjoy.

I'm a nerd at heart and always imagined spending hours engrossed in financial analysis and then handing the results to someone else to present—because that part was terrifying. But it also seemed fun and empowering. Then, somehow, I found myself leaning in the direction that allowed me to engage with people and leverage my natural strength as a connector and communicator.

Years later, I am one of the few women sales leaders in my organization and feel incredibly lucky to be where I am.

Seedling—Climbing the First Steps on the Corporate Ladder

In the next few pages, I want to share my thoughts on navigating the frequently confusing and opaque world of corporate career ladders, what has helped me succeed, and what I have learned from some pretty amazing people along the way.

If you are in that world or interested in pursuing it, I hope this chapter spotlights some ideas for you to try out. Pick and choose what calls out to you and rise up like a sunflower toward the bright sun of your authentic journey!

Starting in the corporate world can be both exciting and intimidating, especially as a woman surrounded by male bosses and executives. In my first job as an analyst, fresh out of college, I had the loveliest team I could ask for. I'm still in touch with all of them almost two decades later! But I was also terrified of making a misstep and not fitting in. Here are the ideas and best practices that helped me figure out how I wanted to show up in this particular environment:

- **Work Hard and Learn a Lot**:

  College is great and all, but it doesn't give you a real idea of what it will be like once you graduate and join a company, especially if it's a larger organization. Does any university teach you about different corporate titles and roles, hierarchies, and career progressions? Mine sure did not. Try to keep an open mind and ask lots of questions when you begin your career. After all, a seedling needs water and nutrients; you'll grow by absorbing information! Don't be embarrassed by not understanding as much as you want to; you are exactly in the career stage you are supposed to be. Not everything will make sense, and some (or many) aspects of your job might seem boring or disconnected from your actual life. Stay curious and try to make connections between smaller parts of your job as much as possible to find the larger context.

- **Take Initiative**:

Not every team and role allow for it, but proactively learning is a great way to gain new skills and advance your career. Come up with suggestions for an easier way to consolidate several reports into one and create a summary page to help others absorb the content better, for instance. Finding new ways to be more efficient makes every manager happy, not just a particularly nerdy one like me! Don't worry if your suggestions get turned down or revised, either. Just the fact that you tried is appreciated.

- **Make Your Manager Look Good**:

Figure out your direct manager's goals and how their superior measures them, then try to connect your job and those measurements. We are all just people, even the executive, who might sometimes seem intimidating (and slightly like a corporate cyborg). Pretty much everyone has a boss. Your direct manager's ability to grow their career and support their family usually depends on how their superior views their team's results.

Early in my career, I was part of a team putting together executive summaries of our financial results and competitive information for the company's top leaders. I decided to really zero in on how our chief investment officer liked to consume his information. In their case, bullet points, fewer words, and specific number formatting. I ensured that my manager, Tom, didn't have to spend extra time on it, which made him appear he could get tasks done in half the time and helped earn him a well-deserved promotion down the line. Tom has supported and advised me ever since, even though we haven't worked together in a really long time. He's done well, mostly because he's just a wonderful person, but I hope my work helped him succeed, too! I'm all about win-win scenarios so each of us can grow.

Sunflower—Create Opportunities and Grow into New Roles

- **Make Connections**:

In corporate speak, "make connections" means "build key relationships with stakeholders inside and outside the company." As you move through different roles or your team changes, you will meet more and more people. Your network will grow if you interact with clients, vendors, or competitors. Don't force yourself to make friends with people you don't like, but do work with your natural interests and commonalities with those you meet. What's the easiest way to connect with someone? Find a fact about them or their job you think is interesting and ask them lots of questions. Everyone enjoys talking about themselves and is always flattered when someone wants to know more. Don't do this because you immediately want something from the other person; just form those relationships and see if you can help each other in the future. Remember, win-win!

Most importantly, find your tribe of close friends and colleagues, and stick with them. Good people enjoy seeing others succeed, so don't worry if you can't reciprocate your help at the time. Just stay connected to those you really like. Great people are everywhere; if you don't see them in your proximity, it is likely time to make a change.

- **Focus on Your Strengths, Not Weaknesses**:

For some reason, I was obsessed with figuring out how project management works, which goes against all my natural tendencies. To be fair, I do find it fascinating. Yet, I have absolutely no interest in creating a project plan myself and was miserable when I put myself in a position to do that. However, many amazing people are so skilled in it and enjoy it. I am amazed at my friend Jennifer, who rules over a group of unruly IT guys and channels all their chaos into a comprehensible plan like the absolute queen she is.

Fortunately, or unfortunately, that's just not me. I didn't start to really grow in my career until I admitted to myself that it was fine to be who I am and work in my strengths to sharpen them. Besides, being able to engage people and make connections between seemingly varied ideas is part of what makes me unique.

Each sunflower is different in its own way. Find what excites you and what you are good at. Spend time in that area as much as possible, and new opportunities will show up for you.

- **The Biggest Secret Is to Like Your Job**:

You won't ever love all aspects of your job, but focus on what and who you enjoy. Do this, and new opportunities will unfold in front of you. Tony Robbins said, "Where your focus goes, your energy flows." It is so much fun to commiserate with your co-workers and friends about whatever is annoying you that day, isn't it? Just make sure that does not outweigh the positives you talk or think about.

I am a ninja at finding the positive aspect in almost anything and letting it take over. Annoying project? It can be done quickly, and I can forget about it afterward. Work trip that involves a 6-hour drive from Lincoln, Nebraska, to Springfield, Missouri, in mid-December? I get to do it with my favorite co-worker and listen to a fun audiobook on the way (plus, it makes for a good story). Difficult client problem? I make it my mission to figure out how to fix it and then get bragging rights as the person who did the impossible.

Let's also be realistic here. If you have been in the same position for a while, tried different resolutions, or explored other options and are still unhappy, you must push yourself to make a change. That means potentially a different role, company, and/or location. There just is no way around it, and you will know that you made the right call once you plant yourself in an environment that is a better fit for you.

Nurturing New Plants—Team Leadership and Training

As you grow and move up the ladder, you may become the leader of a team or at least one person. Then what?

- **Teamwork Makes the Dream Work**:

  I stole that quote from an incredible colleague of mine (who took it from John C. Maxwell) when I started my current role almost five years ago. Ann was the only woman on a team of 22 men nationwide. I still joke that I want to be her when I grow up, but I'm not joking . . . . She is fierce, kind, and successful, and her team is always loyal to her and focused on their collective success.

Ann taught me that your success as a leader depends on how well your team is doing. In most cases, the way to create sustainable performance is to understand what motivates each team member and incentivize them with it. Bullying, yelling, or talking down to people only works for so long or not at all. I've seen too many departments lose valuable team members because they were not cared for or listened to. Alternatively, people have stayed in positions because they enjoy working there so much, despite a higher paying role available elsewhere.

Once you figure out what motivates your team members, you also need to understand their strengths and weaknesses. If you can, allocate specific tasks to help people stretch and learn where necessary while keeping assignments enjoyable. Don't make the introvert make all the cold calls if you have an extrovert sitting right there (unless the introvert has specifically told you they'd like to push themselves in that direction, of course). Forcing people outside their comfort zones in high-stress situations might make them so unhappy that they leave or mentally check out.

- **Recognize Effort and Accomplishments (but also focus on accountability):**

I love recognizing people for their accomplishments, even if they seem small—not just on my team, but this applies to anyone I work with. A small gesture like sending a note to a different team member's manager to tell them they did a great job goes a long way. Doing so is easily forgotten in the day-to-day grind, and we frequently think that our teams already know what a fabulous job they are doing. Even if they do, they will love the words of encouragement or positive feedback! There is nothing easier and more impactful you can do as a leader.

Recognition goes hand in hand with accountability. I'm pretty good at admitting when I've made a mistake or forgotten to send an e-mail I promised (if my team reads this, let me know if that's accurate!). I expect the same from the people I work with. Things will inevitably go wrong. What makes a difference is focusing on a solution first and then figuring out how to prevent it from happening again. That's where accountability comes in. Surround yourself with a team that will own their mistakes, be open to feedback, and learn from them. Then empower them to do things independently and keep an open line of communication. As long as the team talks to each other and is not afraid to catch issues early, you will all be unstoppable, even if a mistake is made.

- **Support Your Team's Long-Term Goals**:

One of the most short-sighted approaches I have seen leaders take with their team members is trying to hold someone back from pursuing an exciting new role because they just want to keep that person on the team. It will always backfire, I promise you. Everything evolves and changes, and so will your team. Learn every member's dreams and ambitions, then create a plan to support them. We are all people, not corporate robots. What makes good people exceptional at their jobs is connecting their daily work to a larger purpose and seeing themselves progress toward their goals. Maybe it's buying a house. Maybe it's a trip to Bali. Maybe it's acquiring a new degree or designation that will get them to their dream job.

I had very honest conversations with a guy on my team about wanting to pursue more of a portfolio manager track even though we are a part of the sales organization. I wholeheartedly supported his vision because I knew that was the direction most aligned with his interests and strengths and his newly acquired CFA® designation. I even helped him prep for the interviews that landed him this new internal role.

We still collaborate on projects, although he is no longer part of my team. I am so excited to see him succeed in a role he truly enjoys. Plus, when I have a difficult investment question, I have a direct line to one of the smartest people I know!

The Truth About Career Secrets

The secret to navigating your career journey is that there is almost nothing that will apply in every situation. Take in the ideas that resonate with you, and leave what doesn't feel authentic. What applies to everyone is that you will never go wrong by leaning toward the people and opportunities that connect with your deeper core.

Forget about what others might say you "should" do or even what their experience has been; that doesn't mean it will apply to you.

Take chances that excite you, and don't be afraid to try new paths that might come with more risk if they move you toward your goals and dreams, even if it doesn't feel as comfortable.

You don't have to jump out of a plane like me or take on public speaking, but I would love to hear what happens when you push yourself into trying something new and exciting.

My amazing friend Jessica Weaver shared a quote/mantra with me that keeps coming up over and over again: "I love when life surprises and delights me."

I don't know exactly what my career journey looks like in the future, but I fully expect it to be surprising and delightful. I also know I care about lifting up those around me—it brings me so much joy. I want to see others succeed just as much as I want to, and one sunflower doesn't need the others to fall over to grow and receive sunlight.

There is enough for all of us to bloom. Nothing is more spectacular than a field full of fierce sunflowers!

Visit Nora at www.linkedin.com/in/nora-gillis/ to get in touch.

About the Author

Nora works with independent financial advisors and specializes in providing the tools and resources that help advisors scale and grow their practice. She loves seeing advisors achieve business growth, operational efficiency, and quality of life through delivering targeted resources and solutions that match their needs.

Nora has been in the financial services industry for 17 years. In her career, she has focused on building institutional partnerships with key broker-dealer firms, as well as sales, strategy, and investor relations.

Nora holds a BA in Finance and International Relations from St. Elizabeth University and is passionate about supporting and mentoring other women, as well as creating communities and facilitating networking through events and study groups.

Outside of work, Nora spends time doing yoga, finding crazy things to rope her friends into, like skydiving, and dreaming up fun travel plans.

CHAPTER 12

What Balloonists, Blue Skirts, and Your Brand Have in Common

Bethany McCamish

"Am I good enough? Yes, I am."
—Michelle Obama, Becoming

After a long day of conferencing with creative entrepreneurs—all working to better their businesses—I ventured down to the resort hot tub. The bubbles were swirling, and conversation was flowing. I soon discovered everyone in the hot tub, save for myself and my friend, was in the balloon industry.

They sold balloons, created balloon arches, and worked on balloon installations. In between comments about mylar and difficult gender reveal clients, one balloonist said, *"It's just so hard because this industry is SO saturated."* Everyone agreed, nodding so hard I thought their heads might pop off and fly away (catch the balloon pun?).

They all joined in on the party, lamenting how they couldn't stand out and be seen. Was it the chlorine in the air, or did they truly believe that the balloon artistry industry was too saturated for them to grow and be seen? It seems so niche. As a brand strategist and designer, I knew they could certainly build a successful brand, even if there were 100 more balloonists in that very hot tub.

If you chuckled and immediately thought, *but my industry really IS saturated because I am a lawyer . . . or a photographer…* Or maybe you make artisan candles at your local farmer's market. First, you aren't alone. This problem isn't only for balloonists. No matter how large or small your sector, *being seen* can feel like a monumental, insurmountable problem.

Allow me to dismantle that barrier to visibility. Many entrepreneurs and business owners are violently treading water to try and stand out amongst a sea of folks doing the exact same thing.

See, the balloonists weren't focusing on building **brands** that put humans first. They were growing businesses that were all the same—plus or minus their balloon-building material preference.

> **You need to decide now: Will you be one pink balloon in a bunch of other slightly different tints and shades of pink balloons? Or do you want to be the massive blimp in the sky no one can miss?**

Since you might be sick of the balloon references, let me put this another way: Do you want to be an iconic brand like Jenna Kutcher, Skims, Spanx, or . . . not? For your business to do more than just exist, make some money, and then dissolve, you must cultivate the brand.

But here's the problem: Most folks see their brand as "just a logo" or a sexy visual thing. Maybe they would even loop their website, emails, and social media posts into the definition of their brand, but that's not your brand at all. Or maybe you know it's more than that, but you equate your brand to your services, products, and business . . . still, it's not those either, and it is not *you* . . . .

Here's what I mean.

When I say Nike, you probably think:

Swoosh, epic sneakers, Air Jordans, and their memorable tagline: Just Do It.

When I say Jeep, you may think:

Boxy, rugged all-terrain vehicles built to take you on your next adventure.

Whatever you see, hear, feel, say, or text to your friend about a company or business—THAT is the brand. It lives in your mind. And by "you," I mean collectively, *the humans who are the brand audience.* And if a brand lives long enough, it becomes iconic.

> **Let me tell you that all the iconic brands, the ones that have stood the test of time,** focused on shaping their brand **because they understand that this delivers impact, not just an imprint.**

Many of my clients fear figuring out how to build a symbiotic relationship with their business and its people—AKA your brand. But, your people, *those humans*, are an essential part of the equation, although not the only part.

Why the Fear Around Building a Brand vs. a Business?

I have found for my clients the fear is not of the audience themselves. They are, after all, *your people*. You likely built your business to serve and help them. The fear in achieving this successful (hopefully iconic) relationship is in the ability of your people to now *see* a person(a) within your business. And that's the other part of the equation.

This is powerful because when your people see you (even if it's your company persona), they can then choose you or not. And we humans don't love rejection.

So, really, that fear is rooted in vulnerable visibility. This is especially true for women in a world where being seen has not always been a given.

I know this on a level that goes beyond brand building, as I came from a world where women were only visible for what they could carry and care for.

The Blue Skirt

My father grabbed me and told me to come outside. His hand burrowed into my arm as I half-walked, half-stumbled back to the parking lot. He let go, and the blood rushed back to where he was squeezing.

His voice was deep. The kind of deep every child learns to fear. I looked up at his six-foot-plus frame towering over me and tried to make out his face shadowed by hair the color of ravens. He said, "You need to change your clothes immediately."

I said, "I don't have anything else to wear."

He opened the car door and dug through the bag I'd thrown on the car seat on my way into church that morning.

He pulled out the ankle-length skirt I wore the day before. It didn't even match my top.

When I protested, he said, "That doesn't matter."

My mother had joined us now. Embarrassed at the "scene" I'd caused. No one else was in the parking lot, so I assume she meant when I'd walked into church.

She shook her head. She was good at that. "You can't wear things like that. It's too short, and you're too big . . . . Plus, it's inappropriate."

If only I hadn't gone to the thrift store and bought *those* clothes.

My friend and I had gone to the thrift store, and I bought a blue skirt that hit just above my knees. It was so cool. I thought about how much I wished I could wear makeup—because then I would get blue eye shadow to match.

I bought it. It was perfect for a hot day.

This is where I went wrong.

I didn't think about how this skirt screamed "slut" with every ounce of blue embedded in that soft, stretchy fabric. How "inappropriate" it was to wear to church. How much of a stumbling block I would be as an 11-year-old for all the men at the church. How I would be seen as too much.

On a deeper level, I was obsessed with being seen as more than the one thing I knew a woman could be noticed for—a vessel of use to men.

My parents saw me. Their eyes went up and down, settling on my bare legs. A look I had seen many times settled on their faces. I knew I was shameful.

After the conversation at the car, I changed and returned to church in my mismatched skirt and top. No one said anything, but then again, the women at this church were always at a loss for words.

I Said What I Said

You see, I was raised in a Christian cult. Not the kind that lives on a compound. Not even the kind with a commune. If you're thinking Manson Family, you've gone too sensational.

> **This was a subtle cult. One that walks a fine line between total societal rejection and what the world has to offer. It knew how to both be in the world and outside it.**

The pastor sat at the head and the deacons under him. The individual families had a structure as well. Man and woman. Married, of course, plus as many kids as God could provide.

The largest family in the church had 13 children. Their mother, *the* mother walked in a way that made her skirt swish around her ankles. Their father, *the* father, was revered for truly and honestly living for God and producing as many future Christian warriors as possible.

We celebrated them.

The women especially envied *the* mother for having a body that adapted to her obligation of creating humans and carrying out the role of submissive wife.

The women were excellent at carrying things in this church. I carried my sin, my guilt, my V-card, and my baby sister on my hip. I carried the marks given to me by my mother, my Bible, and the shame of wanting to wear that blue skirt. Really, it was the shame of wanting to be seen when I was already too much.

At 15, the weight of it all caused a crack in the tiny shred of belief I had left for the teachings of the church . . . and my family.

It broke me enough to try for something else.

I took an early entry exam at the local community college . . . and I passed.

Getting in meant two free years of college.

It meant I lied about my age to avoid the looks from other 18- and 19-year-olds.

It meant I could learn about subjects left out of my homeschool education. Topics like women's rights. Design. Communications. Psychology. I could learn how humans worked, connected, and built relationships. I was obsessed with learning even more than that blue skirt.

After two years, I transferred straight to a university.

Escape and Estrangement

They say college is an experimental time—and this was true for me—but my experiment wasn't with weed and relationships as much as it was with escape and estrangement. I could not have choice and be *a chosen one* as a woman. So, I chose myself and a BFA degree.

Next came grad school and industry work simultaneously.

After that, I started my teaching career and side hustle: A design studio fueled by my focus to help women show up and take up space in a world that said they were too much. Powered by the strategy and psychology to build visibility.

I turned that side hustle into a thriving design agency with a small team. I later started a podcast to continue sharing the importance of building visibility in a world that has so many ways of saying you can't wear a blue skirt.

Your Visibility Is Hiding in Your Brand

My decision to choose this path wasn't earth-shattering. It was choosing me. It was choosing to be seen.

Now, I know I was also choosing the women building legacy brands, not just businesses. I was prioritizing the women who were told they were too much and not enough. I saw them just as I had desired to be seen in my old world.

I tell my clients, *"Your business deserves to be seen, and I am here to help make that happen,* starting with your brand." Thankfully, even though your brand lives in the minds of your people, *you* have the power to shape your brand to speak to YOUR people.

In fact, you have the power to strengthen your brand right now if you focus on what I like to call the "3 P's."

Promise. Positioning. Presence.

Promise

Netflix Founder Marc Randolph tweeted on the brand's 25th anniversary that on launch day, they crashed their servers, ran out of mailing labels, and ended the day with 200 customers. Today, they have over 200 million.

He said, "... back then, I just wanted to start a company that sold something on the internet. We believed there had to be a better way to rent movies."

Marc Randolph ✓
@mbrandolph   ...

We launched Netflix 25 years ago today.

We crashed our servers, ran out of mailing labels, and ended the day with 200 customers.

Today, we have more than 200 million.

Back then, I just wanted to start a company that sold something on the internet. We believed there "had to be a better way" to rent movies.

We ended up proving that a handful of people with a crazy idea and a bit of determination can change the world.

I'm proud of what Netflix has become and proud of what we accomplished. And I'm certainly proud of "Netflix and Chill." (I never saw that coming).

But I'm proudest of the fact that I didn't listen when everyone – and I mean everyone - told me "That Will Never Work".

7:36 AM · Apr 14, 2023 · **1.1M** Views

You see, the best ideas rarely come to you in a flash of lightning. They make themselves apparent much more gradually, over weeks and months. When you finally uncover that great idea, people may call you crazy. And they may be right.

But sometimes... just sometimes... those crazy ideas actually work.

(I'll be posting all week about my most significant Netflix moments. Make sure to follow so you don't miss tomorrows post)

Marc Randolph ✓
@mbrandolph   ...

We launched Netflix 25 years ago this week. In celebration, I'll be sharing
some of my favorite memories—from the initial idea through the years I
spent at the company.

Welcome to the Netflix Chronicles.

We'll start with the question I get asked more than any other: where did
the idea for Netflix come from?

When people ask me this question, they want an "epiphany" moment.
They're looking for the story about two guys who can't make their rent,
and... boom! There's AirBnB. They want the guy who can't get a cab on
New Years Eve and... aha! There's Uber. Or the guy who gets stuck with a
$40 late fee on a movie, and... eureka! There's Netflix.

These stories suit our romantic notions of entrepreneurship. And they
are good stories, but they are not the whole story. In the case of Netflix,
there was an overdue copy of Apollo 13 involved, but the idea for Netflix
had nothing to do with late fees—in fact, we charged them too at first.
The truth is that the idea for Netflix didn't appear in a moment of divine
inspiration.

It's a fact of entrepreneurship that for every good idea, there are a
thousand bad ones. And sometimes it can be hard to tell the difference.
Personalized shampoo. Customized baseball bats. Customized dog food.
These were all ideas I pitched to my co-founder Reed Hastings. I thought
all these ideas were better than the one that would eventually become
Netflix.

25 years ago, I had no idea what would work and what wouldn't. All I
knew was that I wanted to start my own company and sell things on the
internet. That was it.

Marc just laid out the most important part of your brand
foundation: its Promise. This is your deep belief in something,
your deep desire to make it better with a focus on serving clients
and customers **over** selling a product or service. From mailing
DVDs back and forth to becoming a major streaming service
and then a production company, Netflix continued to keep its
Promise of a better way to access film—over and over again.
They kept their people at the center of their brand and delivered.

If the thought of being the next "Netflix" is overwhelming, you don't need to invent something new, like the iPhone. You DO need to present your product or service through its unique value, focusing on humans first with a basis in culture.

If you can Position your offering through your brand, you don't need to invent; you only need to *innovate*.

That's the second P: Positioning. It's where you exist in the market.

Positioning

Skims is an excellent example of Positioning with innovation. They didn't reinvent the entire wheel. They took a product that exists, shapewear, and decided to fix everything "wrong" with it, primarily size variety, shade inclusivity, and comfort. They weren't going the route of skinny white girls with barely a bump on their bellies. While they certainly had the Kardashian celebrity advantage to leverage and were excellent with their product drops, they focused on their Positioning in the market by making a product that considered what was missing for their people.

Presence

Last but not least of the 3 P's is Presence.

> **Presence means your end delivery of everything your brand offers, from visuals to the messaging and press. It is about your holistic communication over time with your people.**

The best way to illustrate Presence is with bottled water (boxed water, canned water, or any form of water you purchase). Because let's be real, what's inside that container is probably the least exciting thing. But I bet you still have a preference when you grab one from the fridge, don't you?

You decide what water you drink purely based on the brand Presence, aka the story the brand told you or showed you through its packaging. Liquid Death and Boxed Water broadcast a sustainability narrative. If you want a health-conscious choice focused on minerals "untouched by man," you'll grab the Fiji. Traveling and staying in luxury hotels? You're likely selecting the French-inspired options Perrier or Evian.

The point is, if you have a preference, you understand brand Presence.

These brand examples, subscribed to the 3 P's, illustrate how your brand can infiltrate the minds of your people, so you aren't sitting in a hot tub wondering why no one wants your balloon arches that are *oh-so-beautiful.*

Flat out: People don't buy the arch. They don't care about the business. They buy into your brand.

Beyond that, you're carving a path to be seen for more than what you produce or offer. It's your version of the blue skirt.

A brand that has cultivated its Promise, Position, and Presence has the power to infiltrate our subconscious, making purchase decisions automatic because we (your people) can feel seen and heard as humans.

I challenge you to consider your humans first.

Want to see how you score on the 3 P's for your brand? Take my free self-eval quiz to learn where you land. www.bethanymc-camish.com/build-a-strong-brand-quiz/

And, of course, I can't wait to connect with you through my site, Bethany Works®, and on the gram: bethanyworksdesign.

Elevating Women's Voices and Visibility

My mission with the work I do is to provide women with the tools, mentorship, and the visuals necessary to create their own spaces, in the online realm and in person, fostering confidence and catalyzing positive change in their lives. When women can not only be seen but also break free from societal limitations as they create their own wealth, the entire world benefits.[16]

I envision a future where women, who are often told they are too much or not enough, can rewrite their stories and create businesses with strong brands that intertwine with their values.

About the Author

Bethany McCamish, a former teacher and TEDx speaker, founded Bethany Works®, a strategic design studio, and hosts the *Unbreakable Brands*® podcast. Her mission as a brand strategist, web designer, and creative coach is centered around helping women-led businesses be seen and get the visibility they deserve. As she likes to say, "I am the expert behind experts like you." With a Master of Arts in Teaching, a Bachelor of Fine Arts, and a back-

---

16 "Facts and Figures: Economic Empowerment." UN Women – Headquarters. Accessed September 13, 2024. https://www.unwomen.org/en/what-we-do/economic-empowerment/facts-and-figures.

ground in design, photography and film studies, Bethany brings a unique blend of brand storytelling and expertise—including infusing her five-plus years as an educator—to her design studio, podcast and live events. When she's not building brands, you can find her in yoga chasing some chill, camping or hiking with her husband and dogs—which will probably involve at least one tree hug—or relaxing in her plant-filled home with her cats on her lap and reality TV in the background because who doesn't love *Below Deck*?

CHAPTER 13

Escape, Recharge, & Reconnect: The Vital Role of Vacations

Belkys Pastor

"Once the travel bug bites, there is no known antidote,
and I know that I shall be happily infected
until the end of my life."
—Michael Palin

D o you get bogged down with your day-to-day life . . . being a mom, working a full-time job, perhaps taking care of a parent, trying to maintain the spark in your romantic relationships . . . and don't have a second to think about planning a much-needed vacation?

Vacations are more than just an escape from the daily grind. They are an essential component of a balanced, fulfilling life. Vacations offer opportunities for relaxation, adventure, and quality time with loved ones.

This chapter explores the multifaceted benefits of taking vacations, from creating treasured memories with family to nurturing romantic relationships and offering tips to plan the perfect vacations.

As a working mom with a corporate finance job, I was a whirlwind trying to juggle it all. That's when I decided to scale back on my career and work part-time. I was so grateful for the opportunity to be home with my kids (who are 15 months apart!) a couple of days a week.

However, what unfolded next was that I totally lost my passion for my career and the corporate world. I wanted to be my own boss, have my own hours, and be more present for my family.

So, I started researching and figuring out what I loved, what I could be good at, and a business where I could also make a living. That was the birth of Distinct Vacations (my third baby). I launched in early 2013 and finally had the courage to leave my corporate job in 2017. It was the scariest thing I have ever done, but watching my business flourish was incredibly rewarding.

Way before launching my travel company, I always had vacations planned months ahead of our travel dates. The anticipation and excitement for an upcoming trip are all part of the travel experience.

Take a Breather

In our busy lives, we need something to look forward to outside of our daily routines. I am proud to say that I have provided indelible moments for my clients through the trips I have helped plan.

Helping people create their most treasured memories is the ultimate rewarding job, especially when clients return from their trips and tell me all about the unforgettable times they had—that will always be a part of them. I want you to live excitement like this firsthand. If you're looking for some inspiration or are ready to begin planning your next adventure, visit my Distinct Vacations website. I'd love to help you check off a much-dreamed-about trip on your bucket list.

Family Vacations

Sharing new experiences in new places allows you and your family to reconnect in ways not always possible at home, where busy routines dominate our lives. When families step away from the usual and immerse themselves in new environments, life is experienced differently. These shared experiences can lead to deeper connections and greater appreciation for one another.

You may think you have plenty of time to take vacations when the kids get older. However, the years fly by and before you know it, they are graduating high school and off to college.

The biggest pain point I hear from clients is trying to schedule family vacations once the kids are in college. It becomes a logistical nightmare. By then, the kids have different spring break weeks and summer internships. Attempting to squeeze in even a week during the summer months becomes a huge task. Now that both my boys are in college, I can vouch that this is true; I am so grateful to have traveled with them from a young age.

But what is the right age to travel with kids? That is a very personal decision for each family. I would not recommend taking kids on a European vacation when they are very young. Pulling a tired toddler on the cobblestone streets of Florence would not be enjoyable. I took our kids on domestic vacations and to the Caribbean when they were young. By the time my boys were around 10 years old, we started exploring Europe.

I am grateful for those memories. And we often reminisce about times from our vacations. Whether it was something silly one of us did or recalling an excursion or activity, it warms my heart when these priceless glimmers of the past come up in conversation.

My older son spent five months in London this past spring, studying abroad. The experiences he had traveling with us definitely made it easier for him to feel comfortable living there and navigating the city on his own.

Traveling exposes kids to different cultures, languages, and ways of life, fostering empathy and understanding for people who live differently than they do—but have more in common with them than they realize. This experiential learning can ignite curiosity and inspire a lifelong love of adventure and discovery.

One of the things I appreciate the most about planning family vacations is that even rebellious teenagers come back loving their adventures. One family enjoyed horseback riding together so much that I now incorporate it into many of their trips.

Through my work, I get to know your family and ensure something fun is included for each member. Leveraging my unmatched network of guides, drivers, and local suppliers, I can create bespoke trips all over the globe.

Private tours and day excursions are key when traveling as a family. Clients often say how wonderful it is to have the flexibility and truly customize each day based on how everyone feels.

Romantic Getaways

Romantic getaways are crucial to maintaining the spark in your relationship. Most of us are too busy with our jobs and kids to make time for romance. It can easily slip by. My husband and I have made it a point to go away annually on our anniversary weekend. Even if it's just staying somewhere within driving distance, a romantic getaway can help you connect in ways you never imagined. You will rekindle your love and rejuvenate your relationship. Reconnecting with each other while savoring new experiences and memories is invigorating. You may even find new interests on vacation that become a lifelong hobby.

Tips for Planning the Perfect Vacation and Making It Fun!

Planning a vacation can be both exhilarating and overwhelming. From choosing the perfect destination to finding the best flights, it can be daunting and time-consuming if you're trying to do this on your own without the help of a travel advisor.

Additionally, there are many ways to travel, from backpacking to private jets and everything in between. A couple of years after launching Distinct Vacations, I decided to specialize in designing custom, private trips. All the services included in your itinerary are on a private basis (private drivers/guides/tours) and handcrafted just for you.

Why is this important?

Because you should be traveling on your own itinerary, not on a pre-planned program. This does not mean you need to stay only in luxury 5-star hotels, but it does mean that you will always have private transportation and touring—no group tours—and all the components of your trip are hand-selected for you.

One of the most important tips I can give you is to ensure something exciting is included in the itinerary for each traveler. For example, you could tour a stadium if you have a soccer fan. If you have a budding chef, a cooking class with a local chef is super special. Planning this way means everyone will look forward to at least one amazing experience.

There is a lot to consider when planning a vacation. It is essential to understand your goals for the trip.

Below is a sample list of the types of questions I review with clients:

- Are you seeking relaxation, adventure, cultural experiences, or family bonding time?
- What time of year are you traveling? Are you considering the weather at your destination? Is it rainy season, or will there be extreme cold or intense heat?
- How many nights can you be away?
- What are your must-see attractions and activities?
- What are each traveler's interests and hobbies?

- What are the best flight options?
- How many times would you be comfortable switching hotels?
- How many planned activities do you prefer to have versus downtime?
- What is your price point? Don't forget to account for flights, local transportation, accommodations, excursions/sightseeing.

During your consultation, we review these and many other aspects of a trip. Since everything is customized, we dive deeply into your preferences, right down to your favorite wine!

Incorporating a Theme into Your Itinerary

If you're looking for a novel way to make your trip more exciting, traveling with a theme is the ticket. Here are a couple of examples ....

Sporting Events

Planning a trip around a major sporting event can transform a simple getaway into an extraordinary adventure. Imagine witnessing the electrifying atmosphere of the World Cup, the passionate crowds at the Tour de France, or the historic charm of the Wimbledon Championships. These events not only offer thrilling athletic performances but also immerse you in the local culture and the festivities surrounding them.

Combining travel with a love for sports creates an exciting journey where each destination provides unique experiences and unforgettable memories.

Visit a Country or Region Where Your Family Is From

Traveling to trace back your roots and put your feet in the footsteps of your ancestors offers a deeply enriching experience, blending the excitement of travel with the warmth of personal history. At Distinct Vacations, we often incorporate a visit to a special city where you meet up with a local guide for a walking tour, so you learn the history and enjoy a lovely meal.

Imagine walking the same streets your ancestors once did, taste-testing traditional dishes that tell stories of generations past, and connecting with local artisans carrying on family traditions. With our expert planning and local partnerships, we transform your vacation into a heartfelt journey, creating treasured memories that celebrate your family's unique legacy.

Essential Travel Items

From helpful gadgets to practical essentials, these items will make you feel more comfortable and help give you peace of mind during your journey.

- Compression socks are a game changer for long international flights to help your legs feel less swollen and tired.
- Throw an Apple AirTag in each of your checked bags. It won't prevent them from getting lost, but in the event they cannot be found by your airline (trust me, this hap-

pens), you will always know where they are.

- Compressible packing cubes help keep your suitcase organized while saving space. Roll your clothes inside them and separate by type: shirts, pants, etc., or by outfits for each destination. Either way, pulling out what you need without disrupting everything else is easy. Plus, the cubes have zippers to compress them and save space.

Ways to Plan a Vacation

There are so many ways to plan a vacation. You can plan on your own (with endless hours of research), hop on a group tour or cruise, or work with a travel advisor to create your handcrafted journey.

I often hear from clients that it took them six months of research to finalize an itinerary. My expertise is in planning private, customized trips. This allows us to tailor-make every activity to your preferences. We get to know the travelers' interests, and what has worked or not worked on past trips. After our consultation, once you are ready to proceed, you will receive a complete and detailed itinerary in approximately one week.

> **Yes, you now have access to AI tools; however, these tools only provide data-driven suggestions, while a travel advisor brings human expertise and personalized insights that cater to your preferences and needs.**

I offer a deep understanding of destinations, local cultures, and insider tips that AI algorithms may not always capture. Partnering with in-country travel suppliers allows me to offer out-of-the-ordinary and non-googleable local experiences with premium service throughout your vacation.

Additionally, advisors offer real-time support, ensuring seamless adjustments to your itinerary and addressing unforeseen challenges, all while providing peace of mind and enhancing your overall travel satisfaction. Now, more than ever, the demand for travel advisors to plan your most cherished vacations is on the rise. My services elevate your vacation experiences.

How I Help You Plan Your Most Treasured Memories

At Distinct Vacations, we pride ourselves on staying ahead of the curve when it comes to new developments and offerings. Through our extensive network of local partners and ongoing research into emerging destinations and experiences, we ensure that every journey we design is infused with the freshest and most exciting opportunities available.

I personally embark on multiple educational trips per year to better understand how I can plan for you. In 2023, I visited Buenos Aires, Argentina, explored the Puglia region of Italy, attended a wellness spa outside of Rome, hit Sanremo and the Dolomites, and spent two weeks in Southern Spain. So far, in 2024, I have spent two weeks in Sicily, visiting many hotels and villas and meeting with my local partners. This year, I also explored the spectacular cities of Vienna and Prague. Later in 2024, I will be visiting Southern Africa. These experiences allow me to bring clients the most curated and personalized itineraries.

Creating a Positive Impact Through Time Away

Whether you are planning a family trip, a romantic getaway, or a solo adventure, there are so many benefits to these experiences. From creating cherished memories and reducing stress to enhancing relationships and getting out of our comfort zones, the positive impact of taking time off is undeniable.

> **Effective planning is the key to a successful vacation. You can ensure a memorable and enjoyable trip by setting clear goals, choosing the right destination, creating a balanced itinerary, packing smartly, and staying flexible.**

Don't forget that the journey itself is as important as the destination. Embrace each moment and stay open to new experiences. I promise, if done right, you will enjoy every instant until well after you return home.

Travel enriches our lives on three levels: dreaming about the vacation, experiencing the trip, and reliving the memories created.

So, take that much-needed break, explore new horizons, and create memories that will last a lifetime. Your mind, body, and soul will thank you.

Let's keep in touch! Stay up to date on travel news, trends, tips, and destination highlights by receiving Distinct Vacations' Blog in your Inbox: www.bit.ly/BlogDV.

About the Author:

Once a CPA in the corporate finance world, **Belkys** traded spreadsheets for sunsets and boardrooms for breathtaking landscapes.

Belkys' wanderlust started from a young age. As a little girl, she asked her parents to take her on a trip for her fifth birthday instead of having a party. Fast-forward to when she realized the corporate world would not work for her family, and Belkys combined her passion for traveling with her analytical and organizational skills to launch Distinct Vacations in 2013.

Belkys approaches vacation planning in a way not often found with other travel advisors. Each itinerary is handcrafted and designed with much attention to detail to create a client's custom dream vacation.

As an expert in luxury travel, Belkys can plan a flawless family vacation or romantic getaway without you wasting time researching, googling, or standing in long lines while on vacation. Her goal is for your vacation memories to be filled with authentic and out-of-the-ordinary experiences and for all travelers to treasure the memories created.

When not busy designing trips or globe-trotting to meet with her local partners, Belkys can be found on the yoga mat, in the Pilates studio, or enjoying family time with her husband, two sons, and their adorable beagle.

IN CLOSING ...

Our time together oddly isn't coming to an end but rather a new beginning. As you finish reading this book, I encourage you to take some next steps, the first of which is to come back and read this book over and over again.

I love to reread books because I find that every time I go through a book the second, third, or fourth time, I pick up a new takeaway. There may be pieces in this book that don't apply to your life right now but can in the coming months. And you may not need to come back and read the entire thing but one day, you might need to find out how to manage your cash flow better, talk more about your branding, or realize it's time to think about your mental health for the first time in a long time.

Second, I encourage you to build community from this book in a few different ways. One is to connect with the authors from each chapter. Everyone who contributed here is an expert in their field, with many incredible tools and resources to help support you.

I've sometimes gotten a little shy when I've read similar books, thinking that the authors don't want to hear from me. That's not true, and I know that now. I have since spoken to, worked with, and connected with all the authors in this book, and I can confirm that they want to help you—including me! We all came together for this project to see more women succeed and truly rise up and find out who they are.

We women are also focused on building community and are so excited that women across the country are reading this book at the same time you are.

They, too, will return and read this story tenfold, which leads me to the second way to build community: You can discover *Rise & Find* events in your local area or connect with others reading this book. Thirdly, you could even start your own group of women rising up and finding out who they truly are. Take another step and launch a book club, or gift a copy of *Rise & Find* to a friend.

As you turn the final page, don't forget you aren't in this alone.

You and every other woman reading this book are now part of the *Rise & Find* Community, where we believe you are worthy of living your dream life—no matter what that dream looks like.

DISCLAIMER

The information provided in this book is for informational purposes only and is not intended to be a source of advice or credit analysis with respect to the material presented. The information and/or documents contained in this book do not constitute legal or financial advice and should never be used without first consulting with a financial professional to determine what may be best for your individual needs

Made in the USA
Columbia, SC
08 January 2025

230669c8-92aa-4aa0-acbb-2db250838dddR01